Collective Complaints as a Means for Protecting Social Rights in Europe

Collective Complaints as a Means for Protecting Social Rights in Europe

Giuseppe Palmisano

ANTHEM PRESS

Anthem Press
An imprint of Wimbledon Publishing Company
www.anthempress.com

This edition first published in UK and USA 2022
by ANTHEM PRESS
75–76 Blackfriars Road, London SE1 8HA, UK
or PO Box 9779, London SW19 7ZG, UK
and
244 Madison Ave #116, New York, NY 10016, USA

British Library Cataloguing-in-Publication Data
A catalogue record for this book is available from the British Library.

Library of Congress Control Number: 2021952603

ISBN-13: 978-1-83998-141-8 (Pbk)
ISBN-10: 1-83998-141-5 (Pbk)

Cover credit: Giuseppe Pellizza da Volpedo: Il Quarto Stato,
The Fourth Estate, Museo del Novecento, Wikimedia Commons

This title is also available as an ebook.

CONTENTS

PREFACE

Within the institutional framework of the Council of Europe, and more precisely the treaty system of the European Social Charter, the collective complaints procedure was created in 1995 as a monitoring mechanism specific for the protection of social rights.

In the past decade, the importance and use of this procedure has increased considerably, also as a consequence of a number of serious economic and social crises which have impacted, and are still impacting, negatively on the effective enjoyment of social rights in Europe.

The aim of this short book is to explore and clarify the development, specific features and problems of the collective complaints procedure, intended as a *sui generis* instrument for the international protection of social rights, in the light of its evolutive application by the European Committee of Social Rights, the monitoring body of the European Social Charter.

A short monograph cannot indeed cover every relevant topic and issue concerning the collective complaints procedure in depth. The analysis carried out in this book focuses, therefore, only on the main peculiar and the most problematic aspects of collective complaints as a means for protecting social rights. I refer to the collective nature of the mechanism (and its implications from the standpoint of the admissibility of complaints), the adversarial character of the procedure and the particularities of the follow-up to findings of violation adopted by the European Committee of Social Rights. The crucial issues concerning the legal value and effects of the decisions on the merits of collective complaints, on the one hand, and the practical effectiveness and efficiency of the procedure, on the other hand, are also addressed.

The hope is that this book can serve to inform those new to the topic and also be of benefit to those seeking further knowledge on social rights protection at international and European levels as well as to all those who, working within public institutions and administrations, organised civil society and trade unions, deal on a daily basis with social rights and policies in a wide variety of areas.

I benefitted greatly, for the preparation of this book, from the experience of serving for 12 years – as member, president and general rapporteur – on the European Committee of Social Rights. The invaluable insights gained from many years of participation in the institution discussed in this volume and from the exchanges with all the experts and colleagues who over the time served with me on the Committee, contributed greatly to stimulating reflections and thoughts on the topic of collective complaints.

Finally, I would like to warmly thank Henrik Kristensen, deputy head of the European Social Charter Department and deputy executive secretary of the European Committee of Social Rights, for his support and assistance in the preparation of this book.

INTRODUCTION: INCREASED INTEREST IN THE PROTECTION OF SOCIAL RIGHTS AT THE EUROPEAN LEVEL: THE CASE OF THE EUROPEAN SOCIAL CHARTER AND THE COLLECTIVE COMPLAINTS PROCEDURE

In the past decade, we witnessed a number of crises and changes, which have had, and are still having, an adverse impact on the effective enjoyment of economic and social rights by many communities across the world, undermining the capacity of states and the political will of governments to safeguard and promote the enjoyment of these rights.

Most of the countries in Europe have been particularly affected by the consequences of such crises and changes. A major source of concern and problems in terms of protection of social rights in Europe is related to the serious difficulties which workers, families and the most vulnerable people have experienced, and are still experiencing, because of the economic crisis which has endured since 2008 and the 'austerity measures' deployed by some states to cope with it. Inadequate levels of social security benefits and social assistance continue to disproportionately affect those who are most vulnerable, namely the poor, the elderly and the sick. Public policies continue to be unable to stem a generalized increase in poverty and unemployment. The pursuit of flexibility and changes to employment contracts are at risk of undermining workers' rights and safety. Austerity measures and budgetary cuts are placing ever-increasing pressure on health systems, and there are also signs of a potential deterioration in the protection of health and safety at work.

Secondly, problems have arisen in the recent past, and are continuing in the present, because of the migrant and refugee crisis. Over the past five years, millions of migrants and refugees fleeing war, terror, torture, persecution and poverty have crossed into Europe, where divisions have arisen among European states over how best to deal with resettling people. Offering these millions of individuals hospitality, respect for their dignity and their fundamental rights, as well as prompt and effective social integration, poses a major challenge for European states attempting to apply international social rights standards.

At the same time, as globalisation and automation progress, amplified by the ongoing technological revolution and the immense potential of artificial intelligence, it is clear that employment and labour market policies are changing radically, and it is predicted that millions of jobs may soon be lost. Some forecasts go so far as to suggest that, alongside the emergence of new elites, unemployed persons will soon become irremediably unemployable, while the middle class, which has been pivotal to social progress and the development of a social rights civilisation, will gradually lose its impetus.

And, lastly, there is the pandemic. As has been emphasised by the European Committee of Social Rights (ECSR), the Covid-19 pandemic – and states' responses to it – pose major threats to a broad range of social rights such as the right to health; the right to safe and healthy working conditions; the right of elderly people to social protection; the right of families and children to social, legal and economic protection, including in the education field; and the rights to social security and social assistance. 'The major impact of a pandemic and of state measures in response to it on employment and labour rights, both individual and collective, should also not be overlooked. People must not be left without minimum means of subsistence due to the lockdowns and lack of economic activity during a pandemic.'[1] One could say that the Covid-19 crisis has painfully revealed that preparedness for a pandemic is all about social rights. It requires states to guarantee the enjoyment of a whole array of these rights, including a universal health-care system, employment security, health and safety at work, protection for the elderly, solid public education, a minimum income, an adequate guarantee of the right to housing and others still.

---

1. European Committee of Social Rights, 'Statement of Interpretation on the Right to Protection of Health in Times of Pandemic', adopted on 21 April 2020, https:// rm.coe.int/statement-of-interpretation-on-the-right-to-protection-of-health-in-ti/ 16809e3640. See also, on the question of the impact of the pandemic on the enjoyment and protection of social rights, Committee on Economic, Social and Cultural Rights, 'Statement on the Coronavirus Disease (COVID-19) Pandemic and Economic, Social and Cultural Rights', adopted on 6 April 2020, E/C.12/2020/1, and European Committee of Social Rights, 'Statement on COVID-19 and Social Rights', adopted on 24 March 2021, https://rm.coe.int/statement-of-the-ecsr-on-covid-19-and-social-rig hts/1680a230ca.

All the above crises, or changes, which make it difficult for states – especially European states – to implement their social rights obligations, have also put the international systems and mechanisms for the protection of these rights under stress, particularly in their capacity to operate as instruments to monitor the effective realisation of social rights. However, they have also provided an opportunity to understand how important such systems and mechanisms are, and they are making the political conviction growing that respecting and giving effect to social rights constitutes the best way forward to prevent and overcome such crises. This has indeed highlighted the need to strengthen these systems and mechanisms and introduce changes and improvements to social rights protection in the context of the European regional institutions.

At the European Union level, evidence is provided for this by the action plan known as the European Pillar of Social Rights, launched by President Jean-Claude Juncker in his speech on the state of the Union of 13 September 2017, and endorsed by the European Parliament, the Council and the Commission at the Social Summit for Fair Jobs and Growth, in Gothenburg, on 17 November 2017. The goal of this action plan is to encourage the progressive transition to a deeper and socially fairer Economic and Monetary Union (EMU) and to complement macroeconomic convergence with greater convergence in three main areas: equal opportunities and access to the labour market, fair working conditions, and adequate and sustainable social protection. The aim is to step up the work of the institutions of the Union to enhance the effective enjoyment of social rights by European citizens, on the basis of 20 key principles.[2] The European institutions are expected to contribute to this by framing the relevant EU legislation while fully respecting the competences of the member states and taking due account of the diversity of national systems and different socio-economic environments.[3]

---

2. These principles relate in particular to: (A) Equal opportunities and access to the labour market: (1) education, training and life-long learning; (2) gender equality; (3) equal opportunities; (4) active support to employment. (B) Fair working conditions: (5) secure and adaptable employment; (6) wages; (7) information about employment conditions and protection in the case of dismissals; (8) social dialogue and involvement of workers; (9) work–life balance; (10) healthy, safe and well-adapted work environment and data protection. (C) Social protection and inclusion: (11) childcare and support to children; (12) social protection; (13) unemployment benefits; (14) minimum income; (15) old-age income and pensions; (16) health care; (17) inclusion of people with disabilities; (18) long-term care; (19) housing and assistance for the homeless; (20) access to essential services.

3. On the European Pillar of Social Rights, from the viewpoint which is of interest for the present work, see the report by O. De Schutter, *The European Pillar of Social Rights and the Role of the European Social Charter in the EU Legal Order*, Council of Europe, July 2019, https://rm.coe.int/study-on-the-european-pillar-of-social-rights-and-the-role-of-the-esc-/1680903132.

At the same time, at the level of the pan-European international organisation primarily involved in giving effect to human rights, namely the Council of Europe, this decade of crises has provided a testing ground for the European Social Charter (ESC) and its supervisory mechanisms. And it has also offered an opportunity to give new impetus to this treaty system designed to guarantee fundamental social and economic rights, which indeed acts as a counterpart to the European Convention on Human Rights (whose focus is rather on civil and political rights, and fundamental freedoms).

The renewed attention paid to the ESC system and its potential as an instrument for the protection of social rights is clearly reflected in a series of initiatives set up by the Council of Europe in recent years. Most are linked to what is called the 'Turin Process' (named after the Italian city in which the Charter was opened for signature on 18 October 1961). This appellation is used to refer to a series of initiatives – high-level conferences, interparliamentary conferences and public forums – which was launched by the Secretary General of the Council of Europe, Thorbjørn Jagland, in October 2014, to uphold the protection and promotion of social rights as founding values of Europe, all European states and the European Union and to reinforce the ESC system as a key instrument for the protection of these rights.[4]

---

4. In 2014, the Secretary General of the Council of Europe stated, when outlining his strategic vision and programme for his second term of office, that strengthening the ESC was one of the imperative requirements to increase the organisation's relevance and efficiency. Shortly afterwards, in October 2014, he launched the 'Turin Process' at the High-Level Conference designed to restore the Charter to its position at the core of Europe's human rights architecture. In February 2015, the general report of the Turin conference, drawn up by Mr Michele Nicoletti, vice-president of the Parliamentary Assembly of the Council of Europe, was submitted to the Committee of Ministers, https://rm.coe.int/CoERMPublicCommonSearchServices/DisplayDCTMCont ent?documentId=090000168048acf8.

During the Belgian Chairmanship of the Council of Europe, the Belgian authorities, following up in some respects on the Turin conference, hosted a conference in co-operation with the Council of Europe on 'The Future of the Protection of Social Rights in Europe', held in Brussels on 12 and 13 February 2015. This event provided an opportunity for a rewarding exchange of views between academic experts, social partners, civil society organisations and representatives of international bodies and political institutions. It led to the preparation of the 'Brussels Document', which was drawn up by a group of academic experts chaired by the General Coordinator of the Academic Network of the European Social Charter and Social Rights, Professor Jean-François Akandji-Kombé, https://rm.coe.int/CoERMPublicCommonSearchServices/Display DCTMContent?documentId=090000168045ad98.

The third High-Level Conference, focusing specifically on the Social Charter, was held, in Turin once more, on 17 and 18 March 2016. It was attended by representatives of the parliaments of all the Council of Europe member states, the Parliamentary

Besides the steps taken as part of the Turin Process, other initiatives and measures have recently been adopted by the Committee of Ministers of the Council of Europe to strengthen the ESC system. In this connection, it should be mentioned that the Committee of Ministers has instructed the Steering Committee for Human Rights (CDDH) to carry out an analysis of the legal framework which governs the protection of social rights at the Council of Europe and make proposals to improve the implementation of these rights. In accordance with these terms of reference, the CDDH has published two reports, which focus on the Charter system and present interesting findings and practical proposals to strengthen and improve it.[5]

Lastly, with a view to contributing to the process of improvement or possible reform of the ESC system, and speeding up its realisation, the current Secretary General of the Council of Europe, Marija Pejčinović Burić, decided, in February 2021, to bring together a group of high-level experts responsible for suggesting concrete actions to ensure the strengthening and improvement of this system, taking into account the recommendations made by the CDDH and the follow-up already given to them by the bodies of the Charter.[6]

Assembly of the Council of Europe and the European Parliament. The conference was an opportunity not just to give more resonance to the Charter and the ECSR's case law at the level of national institutions and authorities but also to enhance the synergies between EU legislation and the Social Charter, so that the Charter could be duly taken into account by the EU institutions when they were preparing the European Pillar of Social Rights, https://www.coe.int/en/web/european-social-charter/conference-turin-2016.

Lastly, the fourth High-Level Conference was held in Nicosia on 24 February 2017 by the Supreme Court of Cyprus in cooperation with the Council of Europe, on the theme 'Social Rights in Today's Europe: The Role of Domestic and European Courts', in order to take stock of the role and potential contribution of national and European courts in the application of social rights in Europe, https://www.coe.int/en/web/european-social-charter/conference-cyprus-2017.

On the Turin Process, see J. Luther and L. Mola (eds), *Les droits sociaux de l'Europe sous le 'processus de Turin' [Europe's Social Rights under the 'Turin Process']* (Napoli: Editoriale Scientifica, 2016).

5. *Improving the Protection of Social Rights in Europe*, Volume I, 'Analysis of the Legal Framework of the Council of Europe for the Protection of Social Rights in Europe', adopted by the Steering Committee for Human Rights at its 89th meeting (19–22 June 2018), https://rm.coe.int/droits-sociaux-volume-i-eng/1680a0770a; Volume II, 'Report Identifying Good Practices and Making Proposals with a View to Improving the Implementation of Social Rights in Europe', adopted by the Steering Committee for Human Rights at its 91st meeting (18–21 June 2019), https://rm.coe.int/droits-sociaux-volume-ii-eng/1680a0770c.

6. The group of high-level experts concluded its work on 19 March 2021, adopting a report entitled 'Social Rights Monitoring in the Council of Europe: Ways Forward'. The suggestions proposed by this group of advisors form the main basis of the Secretary

But the growing importance of the ESC system as a social rights protection instrument, particularly, but not only, in times of crisis, is reflected above all in the use that has been made of it in recent years and especially in the significant increase in the number of 'collective complaints' that have been submitted to the Charter supervisory body, the ECSR.

The purpose of these complaints is to get the ECSR to rule on possible violations of the Charter in the states concerned, so that these states can be required to take measures to remedy the situation creating the violation. In this respect, it is worth noting that, while over the first 17 years of operation of the procedure (1998–2014), only just over 110 complaints were lodged, in more recent times, over 80 complaints were lodged in only five years (2015–20).[7]

Further evidence of the efficiency and potential of this collective complaints procedure is afforded by the fact that in recent years, it has become the Charter's 'flagship procedure', namely one that is talked about and is attracting unprecedented media coverage. It should also be noted that as part of the measures to regalvanise and improve the ESC system referred to earlier, the Council of Europe's main institutions have repeatedly urged all states parties to the Charter which have not yet done so to accept this procedure.[8]

It seems appropriate, therefore, over the following pages, to look in some detail at this somewhat unusual example of human rights supervisory machinery, which first began functioning a little over twenty years ago, in 1998,

---

General's proposals for improving the implementation of social rights in Europe by reinforcing the European Social Charter system (SG/Inf(2021)13), which were adopted on 22 April and made public on 29 April 2021, https://rm.coe.int/CoERMPublicC ommonSearchServices/DisplayDCTMContent?documentId=0900001680a238c2. Such proposals have been presented by the Secretary General to the Committee of Ministers of the Council of Europe, with a view to possibly decide on practical arrangements for a next ad hoc ministerial conference to be held on the occasion of the 60th anniversary of the Charter, aimed at adopting amendments and improvements in the functioning of the ESC system.

7. All the material relating to the collective complaints procedure (complaints, case documents, decisions of the ECSR, follow-up to decisions) is available on the Council of Europe's European Social Charter website, https://www.coe.int/en/web/european-social-charter/collective-complaints-procedure.

8. See, for example, the Declaration and Decision of the Committee of Ministers of the Council of Europe, adopted at the 129th session (Helsinki, May 2019), Decl(17/05/2019) and CM/Del/Dec(2019)129/2a, https://search.coe.int/cm/pages/result_deta ils.aspx?objectid=09000016809477f1. It is worth noting that, as a positive follow-up to the invitation from the Council of Europe's institutions, as well as to the 'Call' by the representatives of the states parties to the European Social Charter having accepted the collective complaints procedure (see Chapter 8, footnote 8). Spain very recently accepted such a procedure, by ratifying, on 17 May 2021, the 1995 Additional Protocol

and to do so on the basis of its evolving application by the body that has been in charge of dealing with the complaints actually lodged over the past two decades, namely the ECSR.

This, we hope, will help to gain a better understanding and to raise awareness of this international procedure for the protection of human rights (and, more specifically, social rights), which legal commentators took a serious interest in only when it was first set up and during the first experiences of its application by the ECSR.[9] We also hope that it will provide specific food for thought on more general matters relating to the justiciability or enforceability of social rights, and the potential and the limits of international supervisory and protection mechanisms for this category of human rights, at a time when the need for such supervision and protection is – as noted earlier – strongly felt and widespread, at the national, European and world level.

Providing for a System of Collective Complaints, https://www.coe.int/en/web/europ ean-social-charter/-/spain-ratifies-the-revised-european-social-charter-and-accepts-the-collective-complaints-procedure.

9. See F. Sudre, 'Le Protocole additionnel à la Charte sociale européenne prévoyant un système de réclamations collectives', *Revue générale de droit international public*, 100, no. 3 (1996): 715–39; T. A. Novitz, 'Are Social Rights Necessarily Collective Rights? A Critical Analysis of the Collective Complaints Protocol to the European Social Charter', *European Human Rights Law Review*, 2, no. 1 (2002): 50–66; R. R. Churchill and U. Khaliq, 'The Collective Complaint Mechanism for Ensuring Compliance with Economic and Social Rights: An Effective Mechanism for Ensuring Compliance with Economic and Social Rights?', *European Journal of International Law*, 15, no. 3 (2004): 417–56; Ph. Alston, 'Assessing the Strengths and Weaknesses of the European Social Charter's Supervisory System', in *Social Rights in Europe*, ed. B. De Burca and B. De Witte (Oxford: Oxford University Press, 2005), 45–68; H. Cullen, 'The Collective Complaints System of the European Social Charter: Interpretative Methods of the European Committee of Social Rights', *Human Rights Law Review*, 9, no. 1 (2009), 61–93. See also, more recently, J.-M. Belorgey, 'La Carta social europea y el Comité europeo de derechos sociales: el mecanismo de reclamaciones colectivas', in *Tratado sobre Protección de Derechos Sociales*, ed. M. Terol Becerra and L. Jimena Quesada (Valencia: Tirant, 2014), 231–48; R. Priore, 'Les systèmes de contrôle de l'application de la Charte sociale européenne: la procédure de réclamations collectives', in *La Charte Sociale Européenne et les défis du XXIe siècle [European Social Charter and the Challenges of the Twenty-First Century]*, ed. M. D'Amico and G. Guiglia (Napoli: Edizioni scientifiche italiane, 2014), 159–70.

Chapter 1

THE EUROPEAN SOCIAL CHARTER TREATY SYSTEM IN A NUTSHELL

With a view to properly framing the functioning and specific features of the collective complaints procedure as an instrument for the protection of social rights, it is necessary to give a brief overview of the treaty system within which it takes places, that is to say the European Social Charter (ESC) – a complex and articulated system, which has changed substantially over time.

As a Council of Europe treaty, the ESC was originally signed in 1961 and was, at that time, the second-born daughter in the family of human rights treaties adopted within the Council of Europe, after its elder sister, the European Convention on Human Rights (ECHR). Just like the ECHR, the Social Charter arose from the decision of the Council of Europe to adopt a treaty to give binding force to the rights enshrined in the Universal Declaration of Human Rights, adopted by the United Nations in December 1948. In fact, as has been the case at the UN level for the two international covenants on human rights,[1] the Council of Europe member states also opted for adopting two separate treaties: one on civil and political rights, which was the 1950 ECHR, and the other relating to social and economic rights, namely, the ESC, which was adopted 11 years later.[2]

Although it had been in force since the mid-1960s, for a long time the Charter was a somewhat obscure and virtually ineffective instrument. It was not until the end of the 1980s and the beginning of the 1990s, at the end of the Cold War, that the Council of Europe decided to relaunch the ESC. The

---

1. I am referring, quite obviously, to the International Covenant on Civil and Political Rights and to the International Covenant on Economic, Social and Cultural Rights, both adopted on 16 December 1966.
2. On the 1961 Charter, see G. Barile, 'La Carta sociale europea e il diritto internazionale', *Rivista di diritto internazionale*, 44, no. 4 (1961): 629–44; H. Wiebringhaus, 'La Charte sociale européenne', *Annuaire français de droit international*, 9 (1963): 709–21; N. Valticos, 'La Charte sociale européenne: sa structure, son contenu, le contrôle de son application', *Droit social*, 26, (September/October 1963): 466–82; D. J. Harris, 'The European Social Charter', *International and Comparative Law Quarterly*, 13, no. 3 (1964): 1076–87.

idea was both to make the Charter effective by aligning it as closely as possible with the ECHR and to modernise it, by adding new rights, in order to properly take into consideration the individual and collective social needs which were emerging in a changed world. One could also say that, by virtue of the institutional reforms started in those years, the Council of Europe has intended to give a substantial and effective meaning to the principle that human rights are indivisible and that social rights are human rights on an equal footing with civil and political rights.

This relaunch and the reforms just mentioned resulted in the signature of three protocols, adopted in 1988, 1991 and 1995, and the 'revised' Social Charter in 1996. In 1988 came the first Additional Protocol, which added new rights; in 1991, it was adopted the Amending Protocol improving the supervisory mechanism (clarifying and increasing the functions of the Charter-monitoring body, the European Committee of Social Rights, as well as the involvement of social partners and non-governmental organisations in the reporting procedure); and in 1995, another Additional Protocol, providing for a system of collective complaints, was adopted.

The culmination of this reform process was the adoption, in 1996, of the Revised European Social Charter, which incorporated all the rights already enshrined in the 1961 Charter and the 1988 Protocol into a single instrument, updating some of them and adding several new rights.[3]

The Revised Charter is subject to the same supervisory system already established by the 1961 Charter, as enhanced by the Amending Protocol of 1991 and supplemented by the Additional Protocol of 1995 providing for a system of collective complaints, which is still optional, even in the Revised Charter.

In terms of state participation in the ESC system, the result of the reform process has been as follows: today (December 2021), of the 47 member states of the Council of Europe, 43 are parties to the 1961 Charter or the Revised

---

3. On the Revised Social Charter in general, see, J.-F. Akandji-Kombé and S. Leclerc (eds), *La Charte Sociale Européenne* (Brussels: Bruylant, 2001); D. J. Harris and J. Darcy, *The European Social Charter*, 2nd edition (Ardsley, NY: Transnational Publishers, 2001); A. Świątkowski, *The Charter of Social Rights of the Council of Europe* (Alphen aan den Rijn: Kluwer Law International, 2007); O. De Schutter (ed.), *The European Social Charter: A Social Constitution for Europe* (Brussels: Bruylant, 2010); M. Mikkola, *Social Human Rights of Europe* (Porvoo: Karelactio, 2010); O. Dörr, 'European Social Charter', in *The Council of Europe: Its Laws and Policies*, ed. S. Schmahl and M. Breuer (Oxford: Oxford University Press, 2017), 507–41; N. Bruun, K. Lörcher, I. Schömann and S. Clauwaert (eds), *The European Social Charter and the Employment Relation* (Oxford: Hart, 2017); K. Lukas, *The Revised European Social Charter. An Article by Article Commentary* (Cheltenham: Edward Elgar, 2021).

Charter (only Liechtenstein, Monaco, San Marino and Switzerland have not ratified any of these treaties). Thirty-six are parties to the Revised Charter, and only seven are parties to the 1961 Charter, having signed but not yet ratified the Revised Charter.[4]

As to the Additional Protocol providing for a mechanism of collective complaints, it has been ratified – to date – by 16 states (France, Greece, Portugal, Italy, Belgium, Bulgaria, Ireland, Finland, the Netherlands, Sweden, Croatia, Norway, Slovenia, Cyprus, the Czech Republic and Spain, which ratified the Protocol on 17 May 2021).

Another source of diversification of states' undertakings – and non-uniformity of the Charter system – derives from the *à la carte* arrangement, which is a feature characterising both the 1961 Charter and the 1996 Revised Charter.

Because of the broad range of social and economic rights and areas of interest covered by the treaty, the Charter is based on a system of acceptance which enables states to choose, to a certain extent, the provisions they are willing to accept as binding obligations regarding implementation of specific social rights. Accordingly, while they are encouraged to progressively accept all of the provisions, the Charter enables states, when ratifying, to adapt their undertakings to fit the level of social rights protection achieved in their country, in law and/or in practice.

This *à la carte system* does have its limits though. As laid down in Part III of the Revised Charter (Article A, paragraph 1), the contracting parties undertake to consider themselves legally bound by a minimum number of provisions. These must comprise at least six of nine specified core articles and an additional number of articles or numbered paragraphs which the state may select, provided that the total number of articles or numbered paragraphs by which it is bound is not less than 16 articles (out of 31) or 63 numbered paragraphs (out of 98).[5]

---

4. These states are Croatia, the Czech Republic, Denmark, Iceland, Luxembourg, Poland and the UK. Two states that until 2020 were still parties of the 1961 Charter have very recently ratified the Revised ESC: they are Germany (23 March 2021) and Spain (17 May 2021).

5. The same applies, *mutatis mutandis*, to the 1961 Charter. Under Article 20 of the 1961 ESC, states are required to accept at least five of seven specified core articles (Articles 1, 5, 6, 12, 13, 16 and 19) and additional articles bringing the total number up to 10 out of 19 (or additional numbered paragraphs bringing the total number up to 45).

    In the Revised (1996) Charter, the nine specified core articles are: Article 1 (right to work), Article 5 (right to organise), Article 6 (right to bargain collectively), Article 7 (right of children and young persons to protection), Article 12 (right to social security), Article 13 (right to social and medical assistance), Article 16 (right of the family to social, legal and economic protection), Article 19 (right of migrant workers and their

In terms of material content – if one refers to the Revised ESC – it can be said that the Charter is currently the most wide-ranging and comprehensive legal instrument for the protection of social rights that exists at the European level. Its 31 substantive articles cover a broad range of individual and collective rights, spanning many social areas. Among such rights, employment rights – including the right to work and to employment; the rights at work and the right to decent working conditions with respect to pay, working hours, holidays and dismissal protection; as well as the collective rights of workers to organise, to bargain collectively and to form and join trade unions – represent certainly the main pillar of the Charter, probably the most traditional one. Social protection is another pillar of the Charter and a cornerstone in the construction of the Council of Europe concerning social rights. The Charter addresses all aspects of social protection. It provides for the right to social security in its various branches, such as pensions, sickness cover, unemployment

---

families to protection and assistance), Article 20 (right to equal opportunities and equal treatment in matters of employment and occupation without discrimination on the grounds of sex).

It can be useful to note that only three states parties have accepted all provisions of the (Revised) Charter, namely, France, Portugal and Spain. Italy and the Netherlands have accepted all provisions except one (Italy Article 25 and the Netherlands Article 19, paragraph 12). Other states having accepted the large majority of the Charter provisions are: Belgium, Finland, Ireland, Latvia, Serbia, Slovak Republic, Slovenia and Turkey.

Concerning the acceptance by states of the 'core' provisions of the (Revised) Charter, the current situation is the following: Article 1 (right to work) has been accepted by 43 states, Article 5 (right to organise) by 42 states, Article 6 (right to bargain collectively) by 41 states, Article 7 (right of children and young persons to protection) by 41 states, Article 12 (right to social security) by 39 states, Article 13 (right to social and medical assistance) by 25 states, Article 16 (right of the family to social, legal and economic protection) by 38 states, Article 19 (right of migrant workers and their families to protection and assistance) by 34 states and Article 20 (right to equal opportunities and equal treatment in matters of employment and occupation without discrimination on the grounds of sex) by 38 states.

As for the other provisions of the Charter, those that are most accepted by states are the following: Article 2, paragraphs 2 and 5 (right to public holidays with pay and to a weekly rest period), Article 4, paragraphs 2 and 3 (right to an increased rate of remuneration for overtime work and to equal pay for men and women), Article 8, paragraph 1 (right to take leave before and after childbirth up to a total of at least 14 weeks) and Article 11 (right to protection of health). The provisions that are the least accepted by states are: Article 18, paragraphs 1 to 3 (right to engage in a gainful occupation in the territory of other parties), Article 23 (right of elderly persons to social protection), Article 30 (right to protection against poverty and social exclusion) and Article 31 (right to housing).

benefits, occupational accident insurance and family benefits; it also guarantees an enforceable right to social and medical assistance for persons in need.

But the Revised Charter goes far beyond employment rights, labour law and social protection, providing an overarching approach to what are known today as 'societal issues'. This includes, for example, the right to protection of health, the right to housing, the protection of the family, the protection and education of children and young persons, the right of persons with disabilities to social integration and participation in the life of the community, the right to protection against poverty and social exclusion (which requires states to adopt a global and coordinated approach to fighting poverty and social exclusion). And it is worth stressing that the Charter guarantees all the above rights in a non-discriminatory way. Non-discrimination not only is guaranteed in matters of employment and between men and women but is also a fundamental principle which indeed applies to all the rights of the ESC. Accordingly, under Article E, the Charter applies regardless of race, sex, age, colour, language, religion, opinions, national origin, social background, state of health or association with a national minority. And it is clear from Article E that this list of grounds is not to be intended as exhaustive.

Therefore, from the standpoint of persons protected, it is correct to say that the Charter, more than any other European normative instrument, takes care of the essential social needs of individuals in their daily lives and that the common rationale of all its provisions is the assumption that human beings must have the right to enjoy decent living conditions as members of the organised community in which they live: conditions such as to allow for them to live in dignity, rather than merely survive. At the same time, from the standpoint of the political and legal commitment required by states parties, it can be said that the ESC, more than any other European or international instrument, pushes states to provide themselves with an advanced and efficient public welfare system.

Chapter 2

FOUNDATIONS AND RATIONALE OF THE COLLECTIVE COMPLAINTS PROCEDURE WITHIN THE EUROPEAN SOCIAL CHARTER SYSTEM

The European Social Charter (ESC) is not just a 'declaration of rights' or a catalogue of rights that states declare to uphold or which they attempt to promote. It also provides for a specific monitoring mechanism intended to secure compliance with the obligations entered into by the states parties. This mechanism, which is embedded in the institutional framework of the Council of Europe, is based mainly on the role played by the European Committee of Social Rights (ECSR)[1] and is largely built around two separate supervisory procedures.

One is a typical 'reporting procedure', according to which states parties regularly submit a report on the implementation of the Charter in their legislation and practice. These reports are examined by the ECSR, which assesses whether the national situations are in conformity with the Charter.[2]

The other is what is known as the 'collective complaints procedure', which enables social partners and non-governmental organisations (NGOs) to apply

---

1. The ECSR is a panel of 15 experts (most are lawyers, but some are also economists, statisticians or experts in social welfare policy), with recognised competence in the field of social rights and the subject areas covered by the ESC. They are elected by the Committee of Ministers of the Council of Europe for a six-year term, renewable once. The 15 members are – and must be – independent and impartial. The requirements of independence and impartiality are laid down in Rules 3 to 6 of the Rules of the Committee (for the text of the Rules, see https://www.coe.int/fr/web/european-social-charter/rules).

2. In the reporting system provided for originally, states parties were required to submit a national report every two years on the application of all the provisions of the Charter they had accepted. When various Central and Eastern European countries joined the Council of Europe and following the adoption of the Revised Charter in 1996, the excessive work burden, both for the states, which had to draw up their reports, and for the ECSR, which had to examine them, prompted the Committee of Ministers to amend the reporting system. Since 2007, states parties therefore have been required to submit an annual report, covering only one of the four parts (or 'thematic groups') into which the provisions of the Charter have been divided, namely, 'Employment, Training

to the ECSR directly for it to rule on possible violations of the Charter in the country concerned.

As has already been mentioned, this procedure applies today only to the 16 European states which are parties to the 1995 Additional Protocol and may only relate to the compliance by these states with the provisions of the Revised or 1961 Charter which each of them has accepted.

As is clear from the *Explanatory Report* to the 1995 Protocol, the main aim of setting up the collective complaints procedure was to increase the efficiency, speed and impact of the monitoring of implementation of the Charter. In this view, it equipped the ESC system with a quasi-judicial supervisory mechanism, aligning it as closely as possible with the European Convention on Human Rights, to which the Charter is regarded as a counterpart in the area of social and economic rights. The procedure was also intended to 'increase participation by management and labour and non-governmental organisations. The way in which the machinery as a whole functions can only be enhanced by the greater interest that these bodies may be expected to show in the Charter'.[3]

It is also worth noting that the idea of introducing a system of collective complaints was based in part on the supervisory procedure set up in 1951 by the International Labour Organization (ILO) to guarantee compliance with the principles of freedom of association and collective bargaining – a procedure rooted in the ILO institutional framework and centred on the role played by the Committee on Freedom of Association.[4]

However, there are major differences between the two procedures in terms of both the nature and composition of the two supervisory bodies (the Committee on Freedom of Association, on the one hand, and the ECSR, on the other) and the type of functions they exercise.

Whereas the ECSR is a body made up exclusively of independent and impartial members (elected by the Committee of Ministers of the Council of Europe), the Committee on Freedom of Association reflects the tripartite nature of the

---

and Equal Opportunities' (Group 1), 'Health, Social Security and Social Protection' (Group 2), 'Labour Rights' (Group 3) and 'Children, Families and Migrants' (Group 4).

3. *Explanatory Report to the Additional Protocol to the European Social Charter Providing for a System of Collective Complaints*, Strasbourg, 9 November 1995, paragraph 2, https://rm.coe.int/ CoERMPublicCommonSearchServices/DisplayDCTMContent?documentId=09000 016800cb5ec.

4. See *Explanatory Report*, paragraph 1. The Committee on Freedom of Association has been set up to examine complaints filed by employers' or workers' organisations against an ILO member state for violations of the principles protected by ILO Convention no. 87 (on freedom of association and protection of the right to organise) and no. 98 (on the right to organise and collective bargaining). On the Committee on Freedom of Association, see B. Gernigon, 'La protection de la liberté syndicale par l'OIT: une expérience de cinquante années', *Revue belge de droit international*, 33, no. 1 (2000), 12–25.

ILO, being made up of three government representatives, three employers' representatives and three workers' representatives, plus an independent chair.

In addition, whereas the main functions of the Committee on Freedom of Association are to establish a dialogue with the country concerned and hence, where necessary, direct contacts with government officials and social partners and to make recommendations on ways of remedying a problematic situation with regard to freedom of association or collective bargaining, the function of the ECSR in the context of the collective complaints procedure is, as we shall see below, much more jurisdictional because it has to rule 'as to whether or not the Contracting Party concerned has ensured the satisfactory application of the provision of the Charter referred to in the complaint' (Article 8, paragraph 1, of the 1995 Protocol) and monitor the action taken by the states concerned on its decisions, to confirm whether or not the situation under examination has been brought into conformity with the Charter.

Therefore, the common feature of the two procedures – which backs up the argument that the 1995 Protocol has drawn inspiration from the ILO system – consists mostly of the collective nature of the complaints which the supervisory body is called on to examine.

In the case of the 1995 Protocol to the ESC, this collective nature is reflected primarily in terms of legal standing before the ECSR. As has been mentioned, only certain collective bodies have the right to lodge complaints relating to the provisions of the ESC (more precisely, the numbered articles and paragraphs included in Part II of the Charter).

Under Article 1 of the 1995 Protocol, the bodies concerned are as follows: international workers' or employers' organisations (international social partners), international non-governmental organisations (INGOs) which have consultative status with the Council of Europe, and national social partners.

In practice, the international social partners concerned are two employers' organisations (the International Organisation of Employers and Business Europe) and a workers' organisation (the European Trade Union Confederation).

As to INGOs, these must both enjoy consultative status with the Council of Europe and be registered on a specific list drawn up by the so-called Governmental Committee.[5] Currently (as of 1 January 2021),

---

5. Apart from this, the 'Governmental Committee', which is made up of ministerial officials of states which have ratified the Charter (1961 version and 1996 revised version), does not intervene in the collective complaints procedure. It does play quite a major role, on the contrary, in the reporting procedure. Under Article 23, paragraph 3, of the 1961 Charter, as amended by the Protocol of 1991, it prepares:

the decisions of the Committee of Ministers. In particular, in the light of the reports of the Committee of Independent Experts [i.e., the ECSR] and of the Contracting Parties, it shall select, giving reasons for its choice, on the basis of social, economic and other

62 INGOs are registered on this list. Registration lasts four years and is renewable.[6]

As to *national* social partners, Article 1 of the 1995 Protocol refers to 'representative national organisations of employers and trade unions within the jurisdiction of the Contracting Party against which they have lodged a complaint'. National social partners may therefore file complaints against only 'their own' state, that is, the state party to the Protocol in which they are based.

In addition, any state party to the Protocol may grant representative *national* NGOs within its jurisdiction the right to lodge complaints against it. However, to date, of the 16 states parties, only Finland has done so.

The fact of having assigned the right to lodge complaints only to some collective bodies implies that the complaints procedure provided for under the Charter system, unlike that for applications to the European Court of Human Rights, is not open to individual petitions. Individuals or natural persons may not lodge complaints with the ECSR, even if they allege that they have been victims of a violation of the Charter committed by a state party to the Protocol of which they are nationals or within whose jurisdiction they fall.

This impossibility clearly highlights the other key aspect of the collective nature of the complaints on which the ECSR is expected to rule, namely, the fact that complaints 'may only raise questions concerning non-compliance of a state's law or practice with one of the provisions of the Charter. *Individual situations may not be submitted*'.[7]

This means that the procedure cannot be used to submit individual cases of violations of social rights to the ECSR or to request it to assess violations of the rights of individuals or to declare that a state is under an obligation to remedy a violation suffered by individually identified victims.[8]

---

policy considerations the situations which should, in its view, be the subject of recommendations to each Contracting Party concerned is charged with selecting, on the basis of social and economic policy considerations and giving reasons for its choice, situations which should, in its view, be the subject of recommendations from the Committee of Ministers of the Council of Europe to each Contracting Party concerned.

6. The list of INGOs authorised to file collective complaints is available at https://rm.coe.int/gc-2019-18-rev-bil-list-ingos-16-12-2019/16809947ba.

7. *Explanatory Report*, paragraph 31 (emphasis added).

8. The incompatibility of this approach with the *raison d'être* and purpose of the collective complaints procedure was spelt out by the ECSR for the first time in its decision on the admissibility of complaint no. 29/2005, *SAIGI-Syndicat des Hauts Fonctionnaires v. France*. In this complaint, the French trade union complained of an alleged violation of Article 5 of the Revised Charter (on the right to organise) basing its arguments solely on a series of infringements of the rights of the president and the Secretary General of the complainant organisation. It was alleged that these infringements had arisen from penalties imposed on them and breaches of their rights to a fair trial and to an effective remedy, and of their freedom of assembly and association, as laid down in Articles 6,

Therefore, it can be said that the collective nature of the procedure is reflected not just in the fact that legal standing before the ECSR is granted only to collective bodies but also in the purpose of complaints, which is to obtain a legal assessment not of an individual case but instead of a specific situation characterised by elements of 'collective relevance' for a generality of individuals. And the assessment is to be carried out from the sole viewpoint of the objective interest in the satisfactory application by the state concerned of the provisions of the Charter, not from the viewpoint of the subjective interest of victims in safeguarding their own individual rights, which may have been infringed as a result of an unsatisfactory application of the Charter.[9]

The 'non-individual' nature of the procedure provided for by the 1995 Protocol has other major implications in terms of the specific features of the collective complaints system. In particular, it explains the fact that an organisation may lodge a complaint without necessarily being the victim of the alleged violation and – above all – without all domestic remedies being exhausted, even where these exist.[10]

What is more, the quite unique nature of these collective, non-individual, complaints calling for the application of the Charter makes it very improbable, in practice, that the matter on which a complaint has been lodged before the ECSR has already been submitted to another international body (or is

---

13 and 11 of the European Convention on Human Rights. The ECSR noted as follows: 'The complaint does not pertain to the rules applicable in a country but rather to the manner in which those rules are being applied to a particular case by way of procedures that were brought over a period of 8 years before administrative and criminal courts as well as disciplinary bodies. This, in the present case, does not fall within the remit of the Committee.' For these reasons, the Committee declared the complaint inadmissible (*SAIGI-Syndicat des Hauts Fonctionnaires v. France*, complaint no. 29/2005, decision on admissibility of 14 June 2005, §§ 8 and 9).

9. Of course, this does not mean, as the ECSR has pointed out, that the specific situation to which the collective complaint relates cannot be illustrated by individual cases. See in this respect the decision on the admissibility of the complaint *International Federation of Human Rights v. Ireland*, complaint no. 42/2007, of 16 October 2007. In this case, which related to a problem of discrimination in access to a free travel scheme for old-age pensioners not permanently resident in Ireland, in which the complainant organisation referred primarily to the case of a certain Ms Waddington, the Irish government argued that the complaint seemed to be defending the rights of one specific individual and that this was incompatible with the objective of the collective complaints system. The Committee, however, declared the complaint admissible observing that 'it is abundantly clear from the complaint that it is of a *general nature*, addressing *the application in general by Ireland* of the Charter provisions concerned. *Exemplifying issues at stake by way of individual cases in no way alters this*' (§11, emphasis added).

10. The latter point is not only expressly mentioned in the *Explanatory Report* to the Protocol but has also been reiterated several times by the ECSR. See, for example, *Syndicat des Agrégés de l'Enseignement Supérieur (SAGES) v. France*, complaint no. 26/2004, decision on

currently being examined by such a body). In any case, the *Explanatory Report* to the Protocol clarifies that it was agreed that 'a complaint may be declared admissible even if a similar case has already been submitted to another national or international body' – a point which the ECSR has had occasion to reiterate and apply in practice.[11]

---

admissibility of 7 December 2004. In this case, the trade union alleged that there was a violation of Article 5 of the Revised Charter, on the right to organise, on the ground that French legislation and regulations failed to guarantee collective legal remedies in respect of elections to the National Council for Higher Education and Research (CNESER). In its submissions on admissibility, the French government observed that the matter complained of had been the subject of a challenge by SAGES in the Paris Administrative Court, which had been dismissed by the Court on 20 June 2003, and that an appeal to the Paris Administrative Appeal Court had been dismissed on 9 March 2004. Therefore, the complainant organisation would have not exhausted the domestic remedies available, and further, the possibility of an appeal on points of law with the Conseil d'Etat had not been used (§11). In rejecting the government's objection, the Committee stated as follows: 'neither the Protocol nor the Rules lay down a requirement that domestic remedies be exhausted. Naturally, the Committee takes full account of the interpretation put on national law by the domestic courts. Nevertheless, the Protocol does not require the invocation or exhaustion of domestic remedies as a prerequisite to maintaining a collective complaint' (§12).

11. See *Conference of European Churches (CEC) v. The Netherlands*, complaint no. 90/2013, decision on admissibility of 1 July 2013. In this case – concerning the rights of undocumented adults to food, clothing and shelter – the government's objections were based in particular on the fact that the issues at stake in the complaint had also been addressed in two cases dealt with by other international bodies, namely, the UN Human Rights Committee and the Committee on the Elimination of Discrimination against Women. In dismissing this objection, the Committee 'refers to the *Explanatory Report* on the Protocol and in particular to paragraph 31 thereof, providing that a complaint may be declared admissible even if a similar case has been submitted to another national or international body. Pursuant to this provision, [it] considers itself mandated to examine the current complaint also in the light of these examples' (§13).

The Committee has also applied the same principle with regard to the relationship between the collective complaints procedure and the other supervisory procedure provided for by the ESC system, namely, the procedure for the examination of reports by states. In this respect, the ECSR specified, in its very first decision of a collective complaint, that 'the legal principles *res judicata* and *non bis in idem* [...] do not apply to the relation between the two supervisory procedures' (*International Commission of Jurists v. Portugal*, complaint no. 1/1998, decision on admissibility of 10 March 1999, §13) and added that 'neither the fact that the Committee has already examined this situation in the framework of the reporting system, nor the fact that it will examine it again during subsequent supervision cycles do not in themselves imply the inadmissibility of a collective complaint concerning the same provision of the Charter and the same Contracting Party' (ibid. §10; see also *Association for the Protection of All Children (APPROACH) Ltd v. France*, complaint no. 92/2013, decision on admissibility of 2 July 2013, §10, and *European Roma and Travellers Forum (ERTF) v. Czech Republic*, complaint no. 104/2014, decision on admissibility of 30 June 2014, §9).

Chapter 3

THE ADMISSIBILITY OF COLLECTIVE COMPLAINTS UNDER THE ESC SYSTEM

The basic features concerning the collective nature of the procedure and the entitlement to lodge complaints before the European Committee of Social Rights (ECSR) are of crucial importance to understand the main issues that may arise in the admissibility of collective complaints under the European Social Charter (ESC) system.

Issues Relating to the Admissibility of Complaints Lodged by Trade Unions

Besides the limitation consisting in the fact that the procedure is not open to individual applications (or complaints relating to a single individual's situations), these issues relate primarily – in the practice of the ECSR – to certain 'subjective' features of the collective bodies which are entitled to lodge complaints.

Problems may arise, for instance, with regard to the national social partners referred to in Article 1, paragraph c), of the 1995 Protocol. Under this provision, the right to submit complaints is granted to 'representative national organisations of employers and trade unions within the jurisdiction of the Contracting Party against which they have lodged a complaint'. The bodies in question must therefore consist of a *representative* national *trade union* (or a representative national employers' organisation).

The concept of 'trade union', however, is given neither in the Charter nor in the Protocol or its *Explanatory Report*. In this respect, the ECSR tends generally to rely on any relevant domestic legal rules providing for trade unions that they must be registered, or have a specific organisational structure, to determine whether the body can be regarded as a trade union for the purposes of the collective complaints procedure.

However, the state party's domestic legal order may not establish any requirement for trade unions to be registered as legal persons or to be organised according to a specific structural model. This is the case, for example, in Italy, where trade unions are not corporate bodies with legal personality and are granted instead the status of 'non-registered associations' subject to ordinary law (Articles 36 to 38 of the Italian Civil Code), all of which have the capacity in principle to negotiate and conclude collective agreements, to carry out collective activities and to appear and plead before a court.

In such circumstances, the ECSR bases its assessment as to whether the organisation can be defined as a trade union not so much on its name or its form but primarily on its activities, which must be typical of those carried out by a trade union. This emerges clearly when one compares two decisions on admissibility, one in the complaint *Associazione Nazionale Giudici di Pace (ANGdP) v. Italy* and the other concerning the complaint *Movimento per la libertà della psicanalisi v. Italy*.

In the first case, the ECSR noted that the ANGdP – whose task is 'to define the functions and prerogatives of *Giudici di Pace* in the judicial system, to protect the reputation and the interests of the category of *Giudici di Pace*, to promote professional training and to formulate proposals to ensure the resources and facilities necessary for the better functioning of the Office of *Giudici di Pace*' – had 'made representations, *inter alia*, to the Ministry for Justice and Superior Council of Judges regarding its members' working conditions, including their lack of social protection, and [had] in fact also called for strikes'.[1] Accordingly, the ECSR found that 'the ANGdP exercises functions which can be considered as trade union prerogatives, and therefore it can be considered as a trade union for the purposes of the current complaint'.[2]

By contrast, in *Movimento per la libertà della psicanalisi v. Italy*, the ECSR noted that the activities of this 'Movement' primarily related to the training of psychoanalysts and awareness-raising activities, along with cultural activities, and found the complaint inadmissible on the ground that 'the Movement [had] not engaged in activities that could properly be said to amount to trade union activities, such as participating in collective bargaining, calling strikes, bringing legal proceedings against employers and/or on behalf of its members, taking action in order to support or improve its members' working terms and conditions etc.'.[3]

---

1. *Associazione Nazionale Giudici di Pace v. Italy*, complaint no. 102/2013, decision on admissibility of 2 December 2014, §8.
2. Ibid., §10.
3. *Movimento per la liberta' della psicanalisi-associazione culturale italiana v. Italy*, complaint no. 122/2016, decision on admissibility of 24 March 2017, §11. The same approach

Different problems stem from the other condition set by Article 1, paragraph c), of the 1995 Protocol for organisations to be entitled to submit a collective complaint, namely, that trade unions (or national organisations of employers) must also be 'representative'. In this connection the *Explanatory Report* states that the requirement that the organisation must be representative was introduced 'to ensure the efficient functioning of the procedure [...] in view of the very large number of trade unions operating in some states', while adding that, to judge whether the organisation meets this criterion, the ECSR should take into account 'in the absence of any criteria on a national level, factors such as the number of members and the organisation's actual role in national negotiations'.[4]

Over time, the ECSR's approach to assessing this condition has been clarified and has tended – as was especially the case during the early years of life of the procedure – to give rise to an autonomous concept of representativeness, capable of encompassing a very broad range of different situations.

Firstly, the ECSR has clarified that for the purposes of the collective complaints procedure, the concept of the representativeness of trade unions does not *necessarily* match that which might be applied in the domestic law and practice of the state concerned by the complaint.[5] In other words, while, on the one hand, the fact that a trade union is representative at the national level for collective bargaining purposes has an almost decisive bearing, on the other hand, a trade union which is not considered to be representative at the national level may nonetheless be considered representative for the purposes of the collective complaints procedure if other criteria are met.[6]

Among the criteria that are taken into account by the ECSR when assessing, case by case and on the basis of the overall situation described in the case file, whether a trade union is representative are the following: whether the trade union represents a large majority of the workers in the sector of activity concerned, whether the trade union can negotiate collective agreements and whether the trade union carries out activities, in the geographical area in which it is based, in the defence of the material and moral interests of workers

---

recently led the Committee to declare another complaint lodged against Italy by a national association of doctors inadmissible (*Associazione Medici Liberi v. Italy*, complaint no. 177/2019, decision on admissibility of 6 December 2019, §§ 10–11).

4. *Explanatory Report*, paragraph 23.
5. See, for example, *Syndicat national des Professions du Tourisme v. France*, complaint no. 6/1999, decision on admissibility of 10 February 2000, §§ 6 and 7; for employers' organisations, see *Bedriftsforbundet v. Norway*, complaint no. 103/2013, decision on admissibility of 14 May 2014, §13.
6. See, in this respect, *Associazione Professionale e Sindacale (ANIEF) v. Italy*, complaint no. 146/2017, decision of 12 September 2017, §6.

in a sector of which it represents a sufficient number (in complete independence from the employing authorities).[7]

While it is true that the ECSR usually takes a very flexible and 'all-embracing' approach to its assessment of representativeness, it is equally true that there are situations in which the complainant trade union can be considered to lack this quality for the purposes of the collective complaints procedure.

This was the case recently when the ECSR examined *CGT-YTO v. France*, complaint no. 174/2019.

CGT-YTO is a French company-level trade union (representing the interests of employees of the company YTO France SAS based in Saint-Dizier, Haute-Marne), which is affiliated to – or rather, according to its statutes, an 'integral part' of – the *Confédération générale du travail* (CGT), a trade union federation, which is considered to be representative at the national and interbranch level. CGT-YTO alleged in its complaint that some of the legislative amendments adopted in France, amending provisions on financial compensation for dismissals without a valid reason, constituted a violation of Article 24 of the Revised Charter concerning the right to protection in the case of termination of employment. Very similar allegations formed the basis of another complaint that had already been lodged in preceding months by the CGT (and declared admissible by the ECSR).[8]

The ECSR declared CGT-YTO's complaint inadmissible for the following reasons:

A trade union whose activity is limited to a single enterprise while being affiliated with a higher-level trade union *will generally not be deemed to be*

---

7. See *Confédération Française de l'Encadrement (CFE-CGC) v. France*, complaint no. 9/2000, decision on admissibility of 7 November 2000, §§ 6 and 7; *Tehy ry and STTK ry v. Finland*, complaint no. 10/2000, decision on admissibility of 12 February 2001, §6; *Syndicat occitan de l'éducation v. France*, complaint no. 23/2003, decision on admissibility of 13 February 2004, §5. The same conditions are taken into account for employers' organisations (*Confederation of Swedish Enterprise v. Sweden*, complaint no. 12/2002, decision on admissibility of 19 June 2002, §5). In three recent decisions on admissibility, concerning all complaints lodged by the same Italian trade union, *Sindacato Autonomo Europeo Scuola ed Ecologia* (SAESE), the ECSR declared the complaints inadmissible, because 'it did not have the information necessary to assess the representativeness of the complainant organisation, including any indication of the *specific number of members it represents* or *whether it has bargained collectively on behalf of such members with a view to concluding collective agreements*' (*SAESE v. Italy*, complaint no. 166/2018, decision on admissibility of 18 March 2019, §10, emphasis added; the other two decisions are *SAESE v. Italy*, complaint no. 186/2020, decision on admissibility of 20 October 2020, and *SAESE v. Italy*, complaint no. 194/2020, decision on admissibility of 11 December 2020).
8. *Confédération Générale du Travail (CGT) v. France*, complaint no. 171/2018, decision on admissibility of 3 July 2019.

representative within the meaning of Article 1§c of the Protocol. This applies *a fortiori* where a similar complaint has already been taken forward by a trade union with well-established representativity at national level to which the complainant organisation is affiliated and of which it is an 'integral part'. [...] The Committee therefore holds that CGT YTO France, albeit being representative in accordance with domestic law at the level of a single enterprise, does not possess representativeness for the purposes of the collective complaints procedure.[9]

The assessment of the 'representativeness' of a trade union carried out by the Committee in this complaint differed from that in a similar situation to this (and at almost the same time), in which the ECSR found instead that the complaint was admissible.

Syndicat CFDT de la métallurgie de la Meuse v. France, complaint no. 175/2019, concerned, in fact, exactly the same subject as the above-mentioned *CGT-YTO v. France*, complaint no. 174/2019, and was lodged by a trade union exercising activities in the defence of the interests of workers in the metallurgical industry in the geographical area of the Meuse, affiliated to the *Confédération française démocratique du travail* (CFDT) (an organisation previously considered to be representative by the ECSR for the purposes of the collective complaints procedure).

In this case, the ECSR dismissed the objection of inadmissibility raised by the French government regarding the representativeness of the complainant trade union, noting that the trade union in question was one that was recognised as representative at the level of the metallurgical branch within the Meuse *département* and that affiliation to the CFDT did not in itself constitute an obstacle to representativeness. It also pointed out – with regard to the latter aspect – that it had already held (in a decision on the admissibility of a previous complaint)[10] that 'a regional branch of a national-level trade union was a representative trade union within the meaning of Article 1, paragraph c), of the Protocol'.[11]

In conclusion, if one compares the two decisions, it can be seen that the condition which prevents a trade union from being representative for the purposes of the collective complaints procedure is not so much, in the ECSR's view, that it is affiliated more or less closely to a national trade union of a

---

9. *Syndicat CGT YTO France v. France*, complaint no. 174/2019, decision on admissibility of 28 January 2020, §§ 16–17 (emphasis added).
10. *U.I.L. Scuola – Sicilia v. Italy*, complaint no. 113/2014, decision on admissibility and on immediate measures of 9 September 2015.
11. *Syndicat CFDT de la métallurgie de la Meuse v. France*, complaint no. 175/2019, decision on admissibility of 28 January 2020, §§ 15–17.

higher level, but rather that it is a 'company-level trade union'; in other words, the scope of its activities, relating only to a single company, is too narrow and limited for it to be considered 'representative' within the meaning of Article 1, paragraph c), of the 1995 Protocol.

Issues Relating to the Admissibility of Complaints Lodged by NGOs

Moving on to the other main category of entities entitled to submit a collective complaint – namely, international non-governmental organisations (INGOs) – it has already been said that they must enjoy consultative status with the Council of Europe and be registered on a specific list drawn up by the Governmental Committee. Article 3 of the 1995 Protocol also provides that these INGOs may submit complaints 'only in respect of those matters regarding which they have been recognised as having particular competence'.

An INGO's 'particular competence' in the matter being the object of the complaint is, therefore, a requirement for the admissibility of the complaint itself. In theory, this means that a complaint lodged, for example, by an INGO specialising in the protection and well-being of children but relating to the protection of elderly persons living in institutions, within the scope of application of Article 23 of the Charter, should be declared inadmissible. The same would apply to a complaint lodged by an INGO having particular competence in matters of sexual and reproductive health but relating to the right of workers to the protection of their claims in the event of the insolvency of their employer, under Article 25 of the Revised Charter.

It should be said, however, that in the ECSR's practice, the assessment of this requirement has never resulted in a finding of inadmissibility of a complaint submitted by an INGO, even where an objection concerning the competence of the INGO has been raised by the government of the state concerned by the complaint. The reason for this could be that to date, complainant INGOs have always lodged complaints relating to areas in which they all appeared to be specialised. But it is also worth noting that the ECSR has never considered it necessary to carry out a detailed examination of the 'particular competence' of INGOs, merely basing itself on often somewhat general and vague information from their statutes about their purpose and aims, or their activities as a whole, which, when taken together, would seem to demonstrate a general competence in the area of human rights or social welfare policy.[12]

---

12. See, among the many decisions by the ECSR illustrating this approach, *Quaker Council for European Affairs (QCEA) v. Greece*, complaint no. 8/2000, decision on admissibility of 28 June 2000, §8; *World Organisation against Torture (OMCT) v. Greece*, complaint no. 17/

In other words, the impression is that once an organisation enjoying consultative status with the Council of Europe has been authorised in general to submit collective complaints by virtue of its registration on the list issued by the Governmental Committee, the ECSR tends to consider it to be almost automatically entitled to submit a complaint relating to the rights protected by the Charter, regardless of the specific subject matter of the complaint or the organisation's actual 'particular competence'.

Lastly, with regard to *national* NGOs – bearing in mind that to date, only one state, namely, Finland, has accepted to allow national NGOs to submit collective complaints – the 1995 Protocol sets three cumulative requirements for admissibility. National NGOs must be 'representative' and 'have particular competence in the matters governed by the Charter' taken as a whole (Article 3), and they may submit complaints only 'in respect of those matters regarding which they have been recognised as having particular competence' (Article 4).

When examining these conditions, just like those applicable to INGOs, the ECSR has taken a flexible approach. When looking in general at the purpose and the aims of the NGO in question, or its activities, the ECSR has merely sought to assess whether these were in any relation with the matters governed by the provisions of the Charter mentioned in the complaint. It has not considered in detail whether the organisation had particular competence in the specific subject area of the complaint or, still less, in the overall area of social rights. Furthermore, with regard to representativeness (an attribute which is actually difficult to determine precisely and apply with reference to an NGO), the ECSR has only ever stated that this is – just like the representativeness of trade unions – an 'autonomous concept', and hence a condition to be assessed on a case-by-case basis, taking into account, inter alia, the social objective and the scope of activities of the NGO in question.[13]

2003, decision on admissibility of 9 December 2003, §6; *International Centre for the Legal Protection of Human Rights (INTERIGHTS) v. Croatia*, complaint no. 45/2007, decision on admissibility of 1 April 2008, §5; *Mental Disability Advocacy Centre (MDAC) v. Bulgaria*, complaint no. 41/2007, decision on admissibility of 26 June 2007, §6; *International Federation of Human Rights (FIDH) v. Ireland*, complaint no. 42/2007, decision on admissibility of 16 October 2007, §§ 7–9.

13. See, for example, *The Central Association of Carers in Finland v. Finland*, complaint no. 70/2011, decision on admissibility of 7 December 2011, §6, or *Finnish Society of Social Rights v. Finland*, complaint no. 107/2014, decision on admissibility and the merits of 6 September 2016, §§ 28–30. A typical case of the ECSR's approach to assessing the representativeness and particular competence of national NGOs is that of complaint no. 163/2018, in which three Finnish NGOs (*ATTAC ry*, *Globaali sosiaalityö ry* and *Maan ystävät ry*) alleged that in negotiating the Comprehensive Economic and Trade Agreement (CETA), Finland jeopardised respect for the rights protected by the ESC and its ability to implement its obligations in this regard. In rejecting the pleas of

In any case, the result of this approach has been that to date, there have been no negative findings with regard to the 'competence' or the 'representativeness' of any of the Finnish NGOs which have submitted complaints against Finland so far. Neither, therefore, have there been any decisions of inadmissibility on the ground that either of these requirements was not met.

Issues of Admissibility Relating to the Substance of a Collective Complaint

Other admissibility requirements are linked to the substance and 'groundedness' of complaints, in other words the requirement that they must 'relate to a provision of the Charter accepted by the Contracting Party concerned and indicate in what respect the latter has not ensured the satisfactory application of this provision' (Article 4 of the Protocol).

In this regard, it has already been noted that, because of the collective nature of the procedure, the allegation concerning the unsatisfactory application of the Charter in a collective complaint cannot relate to individual cases of infringements of social rights and hence that complaints requesting the ECSR to find a

---

inadmissibility raised by the Finnish government regarding the competence and representativeness of these organisations, the Committee stated that:

> at a general level all three organisations have missions and aims, and engage in activities, that are in certain respects relevant to values and rights protected by the Charter and its scope of application. Issues such as social justice and equality, protection and creation of a healthy environment, fair labour standards in the context of trade liberalization, are at the heart of the Charter's system of guarantees and may be relevant to the application of a variety of Charter provisions more specifically. In this respect, the Committee finds that the complainants can be considered as representative organisations within the meaning of Article 2 of the Protocol. With respect to the particular competence of the complainants in the matter of the complaint pursuant to Article 3 of the Protocol, the Committee notes, referring to the above, that their spheres of activity, including their campaign activity, have a direct bearing on the protection of social rights and more particularly that they have knowledge and expertise with respect to how, for example, the global economy, environmental issues and international trade agreements may affect the implementation of specific social rights. Consequently, the Committee finds that the complainants have particular competence within the meaning of Article 3 of the Protocol, for the purpose of the instant complaint. (*ATTAC ry, Globaali sosiaalityö ry and Maan ystävät ry v. Finland*, complaint no. 163/2018, decision on admissibility of 22 January 2019, §§ 12–13)

This complaint was nonetheless declared inadmissible on the ground that the complainant organisations did not specify how their allegations were related to the various provisions of the Charter relied on or in what respect Finland had failed to apply these provisions satisfactorily (§§ 14–16).

violation of the rights of specific individuals and/or to order states to remedy violations affecting individually identified victims must be regarded as inadmissible.[14]

But two additional admissibility requirements follow from the sentence of Article 4 of the Protocol cited above. The first, which is somewhat obvious, is that the complaint must relate to ESC provisions which have been accepted by the state concerned. This is clearly linked to the *à la carte* system which is a typical feature of the Charter and enables states to choose to some extent what provisions they consider themselves to be legally bound by.[15] If, therefore, the complaint alleges a violation by a state party to the Charter of provisions which this state has not accepted, the complaint must be declared inadmissible.[16]

The other requirement is that the complaint must be sufficiently well-founded and grounded, in the sense that it has to point out sufficiently and appropriately in what way and to what extent the state in question would have not satisfactorily applied the provisions of the Charter referred to.

It should, however, be noted that until a few years ago, the ECSR was not very demanding when assessing this requirement at the admissibility stage,[17] simply by noting whether the situation referred to by the complainant organisation potentially fell (sometimes only indirectly) within the scope of application of the provisions referred to, and preferring instead to examine the

---

14. See Chapter 2, at 18–19.
15. See Chapter 1, at 11.
16. See, in this connection, one of the first ECSR's decisions on the admissibility of a complaint: *European Federation of Employees in Public Services (EUROFEDOP) v. Greece*, complaint no. 3/1999, decision on admissibility of 13 October 1999. It should also be pointed out that in cases in which a complaint relates to two or more provisions, one or some of which have not been accepted by the state in question, the complaint can be declared partly admissible nonetheless, under the provision or provisions which the state has actually accepted (as can be indirectly inferred from some of the Committee's decisions; see, for example, *Mental Disability Advocacy Centre (MDAC) v. Bulgaria*, complaint no. 41/2007, decision on admissibility of 26 June 2007, §§ 8–10; *European Roma and Travellers Forum v. Czech Republic*, complaint no. 104/2014, decision on admissibility of 30 June 2014, §10).

     A different issue of admissibility, which is also linked to the scope of the legal undertakings in force with regard to the state concerned, may arise exceptionally when the complaint relates to the provisions of the 1961 Charter, yet the state concerned is no longer a party to this Charter but has become a party to the 1996 Revised Charter. In this type of situation as well, the complaint is considered inadmissible (see *Panhellenic Association of Pensioners of the OTE Group Telecommunications (FPP-OTE) v. Greece*, complaint no. 156/2017, decision on admissibility of 22 March 2018, §5).

17. Up to 2018, there had been only one finding of inadmissibility based on a failure to comply with this requirement: *Syndicat national des dermato-vénérologues (SNDV) v. France*, complaint no. 28/2004, decision on admissibility of 13 June 2005, §8.

alleged ill-founded character of the complaint and its lack of substance at the merits stage, rather than the admissibility stage.[18]

However, in the past years, there have been signs of a more attentive and stricter approach by the ECSR when examining this requirement at the admissibility stage. Such signs can be seen, for example, in the adoption of two recent decisions, in which the ECSR declared the complaints inadmissible on the ground that the complainant organisations failed to clarify sufficiently what the link was between their allegations and the various provisions of the Charter referred to or in what way the state concerned failed to ensure the satisfactory application of these provisions.[19]

---

18. See, for example, *European Federation of Employees in Public Services (EUROFEDOP) v. Italy*, complaint no. 4/1999, decision on admissibility of 10 February 2000, §12; *University Women of Europe (UWE) v. Belgium*, complaint no. 124/2016, decision on admissibility of 4 July 2017, §§ 6–9.

19. *ATTAC ry, Globaali sosiaalityö ry and Maan ystävät ry v. Finland*, complaint no. 163/2018, decision on admissibility of 22 January 2019, §§ 14–16; *Sindacato Autonomo Europeo Scuola ed Ecologia (SAESE) v. Italy*, complaint no. 166/2018, decision on admissibility of 18 March 2019, §11.

Chapter 4

PROCEDURAL STAGES, ASPECTS AND TOOLS IN THE EXAMINATION OF COLLECTIVE COMPLAINTS

Having looked at the most problematic issues relating to the admissibility of collective complaints, it is now time to dwell on the main features and tools characterising the proceedings before the European Committee of Social Rights (ECSR), concerning the examination and assessment of such complaints.

An Adversarial Procedure

The collective complaints procedure is essentially of a judicial nature, being characterised by the adversarial principle and carried out, most of the times, exclusively in writing.[1]

Once a complaint is declared admissible, the ECSR asks the respondent state to submit written observations on the merits of the complaint within a time limit which it fixes. It then invites the organisation that lodged the complaint to submit a response to these submissions within the same time limit, before inviting the state to submit a further response. Once this further response has been submitted, the written procedure can be considered, in principle, to be closed.[2]

---

1. It is worth stressing that the adversarial principle also applies to the admissibility stage. Under Rule 29 of the ECSR Rules, the president of the Committee usually 'ask[s] the respondent State for written observations, within a time limit that he or she decides, on the admissibility of the complaint' (paragraph 1) and then 'ask[s] the organisation that lodged the complaint to respond, on the same conditions, to the observations made by the respondent State' (paragraph 3).
2. However, even after the closure of the written procedure, the Committee may agree – 'exceptionally and with good reason' – to allow the parties to submit further documents while still showing due regard for the adversarial nature of the proceedings (see Rule 31, paragraph 4, of the ECSR Rules).

Third-Party Observations

During the written procedure, several kinds of intervention in the proceedings by entities which are not parties to the complaint are possible.

Firstly, there may be interventions by the international social partners mentioned in Article 1 of the 1995 Protocol, which are invited to submit observations on any complaint, whether lodged by international or national NGOs or by national trade unions or employers' organisations. Any other state which has accepted the collective complaints procedure may also intervene by submitting comments.[3]

However, in practice, interventions by other states parties to the Protocol are very rare.[4] By contrast, interventions by the social partners mentioned above, particularly the European Trade Union Confederation (ETUC), are more common.[5]

It has also to be pointed out that when states parties or international social partners intervene by submitting observations, this does not have the effect of making them parties to the proceedings, and the ECSR's decision cannot produce direct legal consequences for states other than the one against which the complaint is directed. These submissions are simply observations on the complaint, which the Committee must consider when making its assessment and coming to its final decision, and they may also be submitted *ad adiuvandum*, in other words to lend the intervening body's support to the allegations of one of the parties to the proceedings.

Conversely, *ad adiuvandum* submissions should be ruled out in another type of intervention, which is not mentioned expressly by the 1995 Protocol, but which the ECSR has provided for in its Rules, and is often used in more recent practice. In fact, according to Rule 32A ('Request for observations'):

> 1. Upon a proposal by the Rapporteur, the President may invite any organisation, institution or person to submit observations. 2. Any

---

3. Article 7, paragraphs 1 and 2, of the 1995 Protocol and Rule 32 of the ECSR Rules.

4. Examples are the observations submitted by Finland concerning two complaints against France (*European Federation of National Organisations Working with the Homeless (FEANTSA) v. France*, complaint no. 39/2006; *Confédération Française de l'Encadrement (CFE-CGC) v. France*, complaint no. 56/2009).

5. By the end of 2019, the ETUC had submitted 37 observations on 44 collective complaints, while the International Organisation of Employers had submitted observations on 7 complaints and Business Europe on only 1, namely, the complaint against Sweden concerning the famous and controversial 'Lex Laval' (*Swedish Trade Union Confederation (LO) and Swedish Confederation of Professional Employees (TCO) v. Sweden*, complaint no. 85/2012).

observation received by the Committee in application of paragraph 1 above shall be transmitted to the respondent State and to the organisation that lodged the complaint.

The aim of the ECSR in allowing such 'requests' is clearly to obtain more information and material for consideration from the relevant national and international bodies having particular competence in the thematic area of the complaint or accurate knowledge of the national situation which is the object of the complaint. The goal is to take a decision 'in full knowledge of the facts' (in other words, making use of a sort of *amicus curiae*) and not to bolster the allegations of the parties, or one of the parties.[6] For this reason, the ECSR's Rules, while providing that such observations should be transmitted to the parties, do not require them to be subject to the adversarial principle or require the parties to submit responses to them.

However, it can sometimes happen that an entity invited by the ECSR to submit observations in accordance with Rule 32A explicitly supports one of the parties to the proceedings (usually the complainant organisation). In such cases, the ECSR does ask the parties – and particularly the state concerned – to submit responses to this kind of observations.[7]

---

6. For example, the following international and national bodies or organisations have been invited to submit observations for this purpose: the Office of the United Nations High Commissioner for Refugees, in complaint no. 69/2011, *Defence for Children International (DCI) v. Belgium*; the French Defender of Rights (*Défenseur des droits*), in complaint no. 114/2015, *European Committee for Home-Based Priority Action for the Child and the Family (EUROCEF) v. France*, and complaint no. 119/2015, *European Roma and Travellers Forum (ERTF) v. France*; EQUINET, in complaint nos. 124/2016 to 138/2016, *University Women of Europe (UWE) v. Belgium, Bulgaria, Croatia, Cyprus, Czech Republic, Finland, France, Greece, Ireland, Italy, Netherlands, Norway, Portugal, Slovenia and Sweden*; the Belgian Interfederal Centre for Equal Opportunities (UNIA) and the General Delegate of the French Community for the Rights of the Child, in complaint no. 141/2017, *International Federation for Human Rights (FIDH) and Inclusion International – Inclusion Europe v. Belgium*; and the UN Special Rapporteur on the right of everyone to the enjoyment of the highest attainable standard of physical and mental health, in complaint no. 157/2017, *European Roma Rights Centre (ERRC) and Mental Disability Advocacy Centre (MDAC) v. the Czech Republic*.

7. See, for example, the response by the Belgian government to the observations by the UNIA in *International Federation for Human Rights (FIDH) and Inclusion International – Inclusion Europe v. Belgium*, complaint no. 141/2017, or the response by the government of the Czech Republic to the observations by LUMOS Czech Republic in complaint no. 157/2017, *European Roma Rights Centre (ERRC) and Mental Disability Advocacy Centre (MDAC) v. the Czech Republic*.

Immediate Measures

Another procedural tool which is not expressly provided for by the 1995 Protocol, but which the ECSR decided nonetheless to equip itself to make the collective complaints procedure more efficient as a means of protecting social rights, is that of 'immediate measures'.

Under paragraph 1 of Rule 36 (which was added to the ECSR's Rules in 2011),

> At any stage of proceedings, the Committee may, at the request of a party, or on its own initiative, indicate to the parties any immediate measure, the adoption of which is necessary to avoid irreparable injury or harm to the persons concerned.[8]

It is quite clear that when adopting this procedural tool (immediate measures), the ECSR took inspiration from the 'interim measures' provided for by Rule 39 of the Rules of the European Court of Human Rights,[9] and even more from the use that the Court has made of these measures as an

---

8. The text currently in force is the result of an amendment made in 2019 to the previous (2011) version, which stated:

    As from the adoption of the decision on the admissibility of a collective complaint or at any subsequent time during the proceedings before or after the adoption of the decision on the merits the Committee may, at the request of a party, or on its own initiative, indicate to the parties any immediate measure the adoption of which seems necessary with a view to avoiding the risk of a serious irreparable injury *and to ensuring the effective respect for the rights recognised in the European Social Charter.* (the italics are intended to highlight the major differences between this text and that of 2019, which is currently in force)

    From the procedural viewpoint, once a complaint has been lodged, and even before ruling on its admissibility, the Committee may now decide to indicate immediate measures 'at any stage of proceedings'. The decision may be taken at the Committee's own initiative or at the request of a party, usually the complainant organisation. In the latter case, which is the only one which has arisen, to date, the request for immediate measures is subject to the adversarial principle. More specifically, under paragraph 2 of Rule 36, 'the request shall specify the reasons therefore, the possible consequences if it is not granted, and the measures requested. A copy of the request shall forthwith be transmitted to the respondent State. The President [of the ECSR] shall fix a date for the respondent State to make written submissions on the request of immediate measures'.

9. Under this article,

    the Chamber or, where appropriate, the President of the Section or a duty judge appointed pursuant to paragraph 4 of this Rule may, at the request of a party or of any other person concerned, or of their own motion, indicate to the parties any interim measure which they consider should be adopted in the interests of the parties or of the proper conduct of the proceedings.

emergency remedy which, according to the Court's consistent practice, can be applied only when there is an imminent risk of irreparable injury.

The *raison d'être* and the aim of indicating immediate measures is therefore solely to ensure that, in the context of a situation submitted for consideration by the ECSR by means of a collective complaint, the persons actually concerned cannot suffer, or continue to suffer, serious harm to essential goods or assets, whose loss – albeit temporary – may be deemed irreparable (namely, serious harmful consequences for certain key elements of life and human dignity that are also protected by fundamental rights, such as health, food, housing or clothes).[10] By contrast, neither the risk of a mere prejudice to the rights enshrined in the Charter nor needs linked to the proper functioning or effectiveness of the procedure are, in themselves, decisive grounds for the ECSR to indicate immediate measures.

This is clear from the cases in which the ECSR has decided to indicate immediate measures. For example, in a complaint relating to respect for the rights of undocumented adults to food, clothes and shelter, the ECSR invited the government of the Netherlands 'to adopt all possible measures with a view to avoiding serious, irreparable injury to the integrity of persons at immediate risk of destitution, through the implementation of a co-ordinated approach at national and municipal levels with a view to ensuring that their basic needs (shelter, clothes and food) are met'.[11] Similarly, in a complaint relating to the housing situation of Roma and Sinti in Italy, the ECSR invited the Italian government to 'adopt all possible measures to eliminate the risk of serious and irreparable harm to which the persons evicted and concerned by the present complaint are exposed, in particular: – to ensure that persons evicted are not rendered homeless; – to ensure that evictions do not result in the persons concerned experiencing unacceptable living conditions'.[12] Still, in a complaint

---

10. In this sense, the rationale of 'immediate measures' under the collective complaints system is the same as that of 'interim measures' provided for by Article 5 of the Optional Protocol to the International Covenant on Economic, Social and Cultural Rights, according to which:

   at any time after the receipt of a communication and before a determination on the merits has been reached, the Committee [on Economic, Social and Cultural Rights] may transmit to the State Party concerned for its urgent consideration a request that the State Party take such interim measures as may be necessary in exceptional circumstances to avoid possible irreparable damage to the victim or victims of the alleged violations.

11. *Conference of European Churches (CEC) v. the Netherlands*, complaint no. 90/2013, decision on immediate measures of 25 October 2013.

12. *Amnesty International v. Italy*, complaint no. 178/2019, decision on admissibility and on immediate measures of 4 July 2019.

relating to the situation of Travellers in Belgium following a large-scale police operation, the ECSR invited the government to

> adopt all possible measures with a view to avoiding serious, irreparable injury to the integrity of persons belonging to the Traveller community at immediate risk of being deprived of fundamental social rights, in particular: – to guarantee that persons whose caravans have been seized are not rendered homeless or forced to live in unacceptable living conditions; – to ensure that all affected persons have due access to water, sanitation, electricity, necessary medical and social assistance as well as to legal aid, in particular taking into account the needs of the vulnerable groups concerned (including children, persons with disabilities and elderly persons).[13]

In view of the reason for which it was incorporated into the procedure and the way in which it has been applied by the ECSR, the drawback or, better, limitation with the tool of immediate measures is not so much that they '[do] not fit well with the character of the collective complaint procedure',[14] but in the weakness of the means in relation to the aim pursued. More precisely,

---

13. *European Roma Rights Centre (ERRC) v. Belgium*, complaint no. 185/2019, decision on admissibility and on immediate measures of 14 May 2020.

14. This point is mentioned in the report *Improving the Protection of Social Rights in Europe*, Volume I, paragraph 107 (see 'Introduction', footnote 5). The report continues as follows:

> Given the nature of the collective complaint such measures are general with potentially far-reaching consequences. While measures in individual situations normally fall within the discretionary powers of the relevant authorities – for instance a minister or an executive agency – this is different for lifting general measures which may even require suspension by the Government of Acts of Parliament. In many countries this would be constitutionally impossible.

> Indeed, these criticisms do not seem particularly apt if they are directed specifically at the immediate measures instrument used by the ECSR. Firstly, the Committee merely establishes in general terms what 'protective effects' the measures to be taken are expected to have and never outlines the specific content or still less the form or the domestic legal nature of the measures through which the state should produce these effects. The state therefore has an extremely broad marge of appreciation in this connection and may decide to take action by means of general measures – where necessary and possible – or by means of specific, individual measures, derogating where appropriate and necessary from any general rules. Secondly, the eventuality that a state may have to decide, according to circumstances, either to adopt or to repeal general measures cannot be considered to be solely a feature of immediate measures or to be incompatible with the collective nature of the complaints procedure. In fact, it is entirely to be expected in the context of a human rights protection mechanism which is designed not to deal with individual cases but instead with situations comprising features

although the ECSR's Rules provide that the Committee 'may request information from the respondent State on the implementation of the immediate measures' (Rule 36, paragraph 3),[15] there has been in practice, until today, no significant follow-up to the ECSR's decision to indicate immediate measures. In fact, for some years the ECSR has not asked the states parties concerned to report on the implementation of immediate measures.

In this respect, there are, however, signs of some improvement, if one considers the way in which the ECSR recently approached the issue of follow-up to immediate measures in examining two recent complaints. In these two cases, the Committee requested indeed from the respondent states information on the implementation of the immediate measures that it had previously indicated. Such an approach could possibly lead the ECSR, in the next future, to adopt findings on whether the respondent state has given or not an appropriate follow-up to immediate measures previously indicated by the Committee itself.[16]

But, in conclusion, the indication of immediate measures seems to be still, at present, no more than a recommendation, or a kind of warning, addressed to the state in question, made in the hope that the government or any other relevant public authority will ensure that the persons concerned by the complaint do not suffer serious and irreparable harm to their life, health or dignity. And, of course, it also has the benefit of contributing to raise awareness, through the Council of Europe system for the protection of human rights, on the existence of serious threats to the fundamental rights of individuals and groups involved in situations which are the objects of collective complaints.

---

of 'collective relevance' in a broad range of subject areas. This eventuality is, therefore, also entirely acceptable if it arises in response to an indication of immediate measures in collective complaints proceedings.

15. In point of fact, in its decisions on immediate measures, the ECSR not only outlines in general terms what type of measures the government is invited to take but also systematically asks the government to 'ensure that all the relevant public authorities are made aware of this decision' (see, for example, *Amnesty International v. Italy*, complaint no. 178/2019, decision on admissibility and on immediate measures of 4 July 2019).

16. The two cases in question are *Amnesty International v. Italy*, complaint no. 178/2019, decision on admissibility and on immediate measures of 4 July 2019, and *ERRC v. Belgium*, complaint no. 185/2019, decision on admissibility and on immediate measures of 14 May 2020. It is worth noting that with a view to consolidating its new approach on the monitoring of implementation of immediate measures, the ECSR has very recently amended its Rules, by adopting, on 19 May 2021, a new version of Rule 36, paragraph 3, which allows the Committee to fix a deadline for the respondent state to provide comprehensive information on the implementation of the immediate measures.

Public Hearings

At least one more procedural feature is worth mentioning. As noted above, the collective complaints procedure is generally conducted in writing. However, the 1995 Protocol says that the ECSR, when examining a complaint, 'may organise a hearing with the representatives of the parties'.[17] Rule 33 of the ECSR's Rules further clarifies that a hearing 'may be held at the request of one of the parties or on the Committee's initiative. The Committee shall decide whether or not to act upon a request made by one of the parties' (paragraph 1). It goes on to say that 'the hearing shall be public unless the President decides otherwise' and that 'the States and organisations referred to in Article 7 of the Protocol and who have indicated that they wish to intervene in support of the complaint or for its rejection are invited to take part in the hearing' (paragraphs 3 and 4).

The fact that the Protocol and the Rules provide for the possibility of a hearing is one of the features which points to the adversarial and judicial nature of the collective complaints procedure and may of course serve several purposes. Firstly, it allows the complainant organisation or the state concerned to clarify their arguments; secondly, it provides for the possibility of direct dialogue between the ECSR and the parties; and third, by enabling a public discussion on the subject of the complaint, it can provide a means of giving Europe-wide publicity to a national situation which raises concerns regarding respect for social rights.

It should be noted, however, that the ECSR rarely avails itself of the possibility afforded to it by the 1995 Protocol and its own Rules. In more than 150 complaints examined to date, there have been only nine public hearings.[18] It is understandable, therefore, that some states have criticised the way in which the ECSR is actually applying the procedure, because they feel that it 'should be more adversarial and comprise an oral phase more often'.[19]

---

17. Article 7, paragraph 4, of the Protocol.
18. 9 October 2000: *EUROFEDOP v. France*, complaint no. 2/1999, *EUROFEDOP v. Italy*, complaint no. 4/1999 and *EUROFEDOP v. Portugal*, complaint no. 5/1999; 11 June 2001: *CFE-CGC v. France*, complaint no. 9/2000; 31 March 2003: *Confederation of Swedish Enterprise v. Sweden*, complaint no. 12/2002; 29 September 2003: *Autism-Europe v. France*, complaint no. 13/2002; 11 October 2004: *European Roma Rights Centre (ERRC) v. Greece*, complaint no. 15/2003; 27 June 2007: *International Movement ATD Fourth World v. France*, complaint no. 33/2006, and *FEANTSA v. France*, complaint no. 39/2006; 21 June 2010: *COHRE v. Italy*, complaint no. 58/2009; 7 September 2015: *CGIL v. Italy*, complaint no. 91/2013; and 20 October 2016: *GSEE v. Greece*, complaint no. 111/2014.
19. *Improving the Protection of Social Rights in Europe*, Volume II, paragraph 126.

Chapter 5

THE RESULT OF THE ASSESSMENT OF COLLECTIVE COMPLAINTS: THE ECSR'S DECISIONS ON THE MERITS AND THEIR FOLLOW-UP

Decisions on the Merits

The act which brings an end to the adversarial stage of the collective complaints procedure is the adoption by the European Committee of Social Rights (ECSR) of a 'decision on the merits', in which the ECSR finds and declares that there has been – or has not been – a violation by the state concerned of the social rights at stake.

Each decision is adopted by the ECSR following one or more deliberations on a draft decision prepared and proposed by the rapporteur, namely, an ECSR member specifically appointed by the president of the Committee once the complaint has been registered.

As appears from the text of the ECSR's decisions, each decision is the outcome of an in-depth examination and legal assessment of the situation that is the object of the complaint, which are conducted on the basis of the wide range of information being available to the ECSR and all the elements, in fact and in law, that are relevant to the implementation of the Charter provisions and social rights in question.

When it finds a violation of the Charter, the ECSR does not just summarise in its pronouncement what the violation is. It also explains extensively in the grounds given for its ruling (which appear in the part of the decision entitled 'Assessment of the Committee') why, in the specific situation to which the complaint relates, it considers that the state has not satisfactorily applied the Charter and implemented the rights protected by its provisions, in the light of the most appropriate interpretation of what these provisions require in such a situation.

Where it deems it necessary, the ECSR may also label the situation an 'aggravated violation' of the Charter.[1]

---

1. The ECSR found an 'aggravated violation' in two decisions relating to the discrimination and eviction of Roma from their accommodation, in Italy and in France. In

Footnote: 1 (continued)

---

the first decision, the ECSR clarified that there is an aggravated violation when the following criteria are met: on the one hand, where measures violating human rights specifically targeting and affecting vulnerable groups are taken, and on the other, where public authorities not only are passive and do not take appropriate action against the perpetrators of these violations but also contribute to such violence (*Centre on Housing Rights and Evictions (COHRE) v. Italy*, complaint no. 58/2009, decision on the merits of 25 June 2010, §76). In the other decision, the ECSR added that aggravated violations:

do not simply concern their victims or their relationship with the respondent State. They also pose a challenge to the interests of the wider community and to the shared fundamental standards of all the Council of Europe's member States, namely those of human rights, democracy and the rule of law. The situation therefore requires urgent attention from all the Council of Europe member States. [...] The Committee invites them to publish its decision on the merits, once it has been notified to the parties and to the Committee of Ministers. (*Centre on Housing Rights and Evictions (COHRE) v. France*, complaint no. 63/2010, decision on the merits of 28 June 2011, §54)

The main consequence of an aggravated violation, therefore, is the request for the decision on the merits to be published straight away. In addition, the finding of an aggravated violation implies that the respondent government must not only adopt adequate measures of reparation but also offer assurances and guarantees of non-repetition (ibid., §54).

For several years, the ECSR also agreed to a request from complainant organisations to include a final clause in certain violation decisions inviting the Committee of Ministers to recommend that the state in question should reimburse the complainant organisation's procedural costs (see, e.g. *European Roma Rights Centre (ERRC) v. Ireland*, complaint no. 100/2013, decision on the merits of 1 December 2015, conclusion). However, as the Steering Committee for Human Rights (CDDH) pointed out in its report, in 2019, 'the proposal to authorise the reimbursement of reasonably incurred costs of the proceedings to the complainant organisations was not currently supported by the Member States, which stressed that this was not provided for in the 1995 Additional Protocol' (*Improving the Protection of Social Rights in Europe*, Volume II, paragraph 139). This is why the ECSR, while maintaining 'its view that reimbursement of costs is in principle justified and appropriate under certain circumstances and an important factor in enabling the complaints procedure to attain the objectives and the impact that led the member States of the Council of Europe to adopt it in the first place' (*University Women of Europe (UWE) v. Sweden*, decision on the merits of 6 December 2019, §215), has decided in recent complaints not to grant claims for reimbursement from complainant organisations, adopting the following wording:

'The Committee decides not to make a recommendation to the Committee of Ministers as regards the complainant's request for a payment of €... in compensation for legal costs incurred in connection with the proceedings. It refers in this respect to the stance taken by the Committee of Ministers in the past (see Resolution CM/ResChS(2016)4 in *European Roma Rights Centre (ERRC) v. Ireland*, complaint no. 100/2013) and to the letter of the President of the Committee addressed to the Committee of Ministers dated 3 February 2017 in which the President announced that the Committee would for the time being refrain from inviting the Committee of Ministers to recommend reimbursement of costs' (ibid. §214).

As part of its evaluation work, the ECSR often gives proof of its capacity to reorder[2] and reclassify[3] the complainant's ground of alleged violation and, above all, to systematically interpret the provisions concerned. It also engages in a systemic and teleological interpretation of the Charter as a whole, viewing it as a 'living instrument', whose content and implications must be seen in the light of changes in actual circumstances and new situations, so as to meet current requirements in the field of social rights protection[4] and in keeping with changes in international human rights norms and standards in the field in question.[5] It also takes due account of 'the legal need to comply with the peremptory norms of general international law (*jus cogens*)'.[6]

The ECSR's decisions are drawn up in a manner very similar to a court judgement (such as a judgement of the European Court of Human Rights) and are adopted by majority of Committee members. Provision is also made in the ECSR's Rules for 'separate opinions' from individual Committee members to be appended to the decision.[7]

---

2. See, for example, *The Central Association of Carers in Finland v. Finland*, complaint no. 71/ 2011, decision on the merits of 4 December 2012: 'The complainant organisation alleges violation of Articles 13, 14, 16 and 23 of the Charter using the same argument. The Committee decides to examine the present case, in the order of the most relevant provisions for the purpose of the complaint, namely Articles 23, 14, 13 and 16' (§18).

3. 'In assessing the complainants' allegations, the Committee considered that the substance of the arguments made in respect of Article 12§2 concerned instead the provisions of Article 12§3. [...] On that basis, in accordance with its Rules of Procedure, the Committee reclassified the complaint' (*General Federation of Employees of the National Electric Power Corporation (GENOP-DEI) and Confederation of Greek Civil Servants' Trade Unions (ADEDY) v. Greece*, complaint no. 66/2011, decision on the merits of 23 May 2012, §6). Or: 'Bearing this in mind, the complaints under Articles 20 and E (relating to the discriminatory arrangements for the management of the careers, including the promotion, of civil servants who have remained in the redeployed corps) should be reclassified so that they can both be examined under Article 1§2 of the Charter' (*Syndicat de Défense des Fonctionnaires v. France*, complaint no. 73/2011, decision on the merits of 12 September 2012, §45).

4. See, for example, *Marangopoulos Foundation for Human Rights (MFHR) v. Greece*, complaint no. 30/2005, decision on the merits of 6 December 2006, §194, and *Transgender Europe and ILGA-Europe v. the Czech Republic*, decision on the merits of 15 May 2018, §75.

5. *European Federation of National Organisations Working with the Homeless (FEANTSA) v. France*, complaint no. 39/2006, decision on the merits of 5 December 2007, §64; *European Roma Rights Centre (ERRC) and Mental Disability Advocacy Centre (MDAC) v. Czech Republic*, complaint no. 157/2017, decision on the merits of 17 June 2020, §133.

6. *Defence for Children International (DCI) v. Belgium*, complaint no. 69/2011, decision on the merits of 23 October 2012, §33.

7. Rule 35, paragraph 1, of the Rules. These can be either dissenting opinions (see, e.g. *Greek General Confederation of Labour (GSEE) v. Greece*, complaint no. 111/2014, decision on the merits of 23 March 2017, separate dissenting opinion of Mr Stangos) or concurring

Follow-Up to Decisions on the Merits

While the adoption of the decision on the merits closes the legal assessment stage of the proceedings – by means of the ECSR's final finding of violation or non-violation of the Charter – it does not bring an end, however, to the monitoring procedure opened by the submission of a collective complaint.

Before dwelling on the legal value and effects of the ECSR's decisions, it is therefore necessary to look briefly at how the follow-up to the adoption of a decision on the merits is organised.

Under Article 8, paragraph 2, of the 1995 Protocol, the ECSR's decisions on the merits are immediately transmitted to the Committee of Ministers of the Council of Europe and to the parties to the complaint, namely, the complainant organisation(s) and respondent state. However, they are not made public or transmitted to the Parliamentary Assembly of the Council of Europe until the adoption by the Committee of Ministers of the resolution relating to the complaint or, at the latest, four months after it has been transmitted to the Committee of Ministers.

Article 9 of the Protocol provides that the Committee of Ministers adopts a resolution on the basis of the ECSR's decision by a majority of those voting. And it also provides that, *in the event of a violation*, the Committee of Ministers shall adopt, by majority of two-thirds of those voting, 'a recommendation addressed to the Contracting Party concerned'.

However, what happened in practice until the end of 2020 was quite different. Despite the fact that a large majority of the ECSR's decisions were findings of violation, the Committee of Ministers had adopted a recommendation to a state party concerned by a negative finding only once in over twenty years.[8] In practically all cases, the Committee of Ministers instead adopted a somewhat vague resolution, in which it merely took note, in the light of the information provided by the delegation of the state concerned, of the state's intention to bring the situation into conformity with the Charter. Sometimes, particularly where the state concerned, eventually supported by delegations of other states, showed that it resolutely contested the ECSR's finding of a violation, the Committee of Ministers called on the state to notify it of any change in the situation which has been found to be in violation but also took note of

---

opinions (see, e.g., *Transgender Europe and ILGA-Europe v. the Czech Republic*, complaint no. 117/2015, decision on the merits of 15 May 2018, separate concurring opinion of Ms Lukas).

8. See Recommendation RecChs(2001)1 adopted by the Committee of Ministers on 31 January 2001 at the 738th meeting of the ministers' deputies with regard to complaint no. 6/1999, *Syndicat national des professions du tourisme v. France*.

the concerns expressed by the government, thus demonstrating that it did not agree entirely with the ECSR's decision.[9]

Such an approach by the Committee of Ministers seems, however, to be recently changing. In fact, after the adoption by the ECSR of the decisions on the merits in 15 'tween' complaints lodged by the international non-governmental organisation University Women of Europe (UWE) against all the 15 states having accepted the collective complaints procedure, concerning the right to equal pay between women and men for work of equal value and the right to equal opportunities in matters of career development without discrimination on the grounds of sex, the Committee of Ministers, on 17 March 2021, adopted individual recommendations on the follow-up to such decisions against 14 states, namely, Belgium, Bulgaria, Croatia, Cyprus, Czech Republic, Finland, France, Greece, Ireland, Italy, the Netherlands, Norway, Portugal and Slovenia.[10]

---

9. An example of this is Resolution ResChS(2015)4 of the Committee of Ministers of 15 April 2015, relating to complaint no. 86/2012, *European Federation of National Organisations Working with the Homeless (FEANTSA) v. the Netherlands*. In this case, in which the ECSR found unanimously that there was a violation inter alia of Articles 13 and 31 of the revised Charter because the Netherlands had failed to guarantee the right of migrants in an irregular situation to social and medical assistance and shelter, the Committee of Ministers stated as follows:

> [The Committee of Ministers] having regard to the information communicated by the delegation of the Netherlands on 16 September 2014 [...], 1. takes note of the report of the ECSR and in particular the concerns communicated by the Dutch Government (see appendix to the resolution); 2. recalls that the powers entrusted to the ECSR are firmly rooted in the Charter itself and recognises that the decision of the ECSR raises complex issues in this regard and in relation to the obligation of States parties to respect the Charter; 3. recalls the limitation of the scope of the European Social Charter (revised), laid down in paragraph 1 of the appendix to the Charter; 4. looks forward to the Netherlands reporting on any possible developments in the issue.

On the complex issue of the limitation of the personal scope of application of the Charter and the exceptional application of certain provisions of the Charter to foreign nationals from non-European countries and migrants in an irregular situation, see G. Palmisano, 'Overcoming the Limits of the European Social Charter in Terms of Persons Protected: The Case of Third State Nationals and Irregular Migrants', in *La Charte Sociale Européenne et les défis du XXIe siècle [European Social Charter and the Challenges of the Twenty-First Century]*, ed. M. D'Amico and G. Guiglia (Napoli: Edizioni Scientifiche Italiane, 2014), 171–91.

10. See, as an example, the recommendation addressed to Belgium: https://search.coe.int/cm/Pages/result_details.aspx?ObjectId=0900001680a1d243. The Committee of Ministers later addressed to the states concerned individual recommendations on the follow-up to decisions on the merits also in other cases. See, for example, the four

But whatever the degree of approval and support by the Committee of Ministers for an ECSR's finding of violation,[11] the most important aspect of the follow-up to decisions on the merits of collective complaints is that the state concerned by a negative finding is required in all cases to provide information, or rather a detailed report, on the measures it has taken in response to the ECSR's decision. And it is to the ECSR that such information should be communicated and for the ECSR to decide, in the final analysis, whether the situation has been brought into conformity with the Charter or not.

This is what emerges from both the 1995 Protocol and its evolving application by the Committee of Ministers over the years. Article 10 of the Protocol provides that the state concerned must 'provide information on the measures it has taken to give effect to the Committee of Ministers' recommendation, in the next report which it submits to the Secretary General under Article 21 of the Charter', in other words in its next report to be submitted to the ECSR under the reporting procedure.[12]

---

recommendations at the 1407th meeting of the ministers' deputies, held on 16 June 2021: Recommendation CM/RecChS(2021)15, concerning the follow-up of the decision on the merits adopted on 20 October 2020 by the ECSR in the case *International Commission of Jurists (ICJ) v. Czech Republic*, complaint no. 148/2017; Recommendation CM/RecChS(2021)16, concerning the follow-up of the decision on the merits adopted on 17 June 2020 by the ECSR in the case *European Roma Rights Centre (ERRC) and Mental Disability Advocacy Centre (MDAC) v. Czech Republic*, complaint no. 157/2017; Recommendation CM/RecChS(2021)17, concerning the follow-up of the decision on the merits adopted on 9 September 2020 by the ECSR in the case *Confederazione Generale Sindacale (CGS) v. Italy*, complaint no. 144/2017; Recommendation CM/RecChS(2021)18, concerning the follow-up of the decision on the merits adopted on 7 July 2020 by the ECSR in the case *Associazione Professionale e Sindacale (ANIEF) v. Italy*, complaint no. 146/2017 (https://www.coe.int/en/web/european-social-charter/-/4-recommendations-adopted-by-the-committee-of-ministers-concerning-the-follow-up-of-decisions-in-collective-complaints).

11. As is stated clearly in the *Explanatory Report* to the Protocol, the Committee of Ministers, in its decision, 'cannot reverse the legal assessment made by the [ECSR]. However, its decision (resolution or recommendation) may be based on social and economic policy considerations' (paragraph 46).

12. See Chapter 2 (footnote 15). With regard to this procedure to follow up on recommendations by the Committee of Ministers concerning findings of violation adopted by the ECSR, the *Explanatory Report* to the 1995 Protocol clarifies as follows: 'Once the Committee of Ministers has adopted a recommendation, appropriate follow-up must be ensured. In line with the practice adopted for other international supervisory machinery (European Convention on Human Rights, ILO, Human Rights Committee, etc.), Article 10 requires the state concerned to provide information on the measures it has taken to give effect to the Committee of Ministers' recommendation' (paragraph 49).

It may be noted that the text of this provision refers explicitly only to *recom-mendations* adopted by the Committee of Ministers (by majority of two-thirds of those voting) to a state party, under Article 9 of the Protocol. However, from the outset this provision was interpreted extensively by the Committee of Ministers, which considered that it also covered all the cases of general and vague *resolutions* referred to above, adopted (by consensus) by the Committee of Ministers on the basis of any decision on the merits transmitted to it by the ECSR.

Therefore, in every case of finding of violation adopted by the ECSR and transmitted to the Committee of Ministers, the state concerned is required to report periodically to the ECSR on the measures it has eventually taken to bring the situation into conformity with the Charter. And when exercising its functions under the reporting procedure, the ECSR assesses whether the situation previously found to be in violation of the Charter has indeed been brought into compliance 'with the obligations arising from the Charter',[13] by including such an assessment in its annual Conclusions (now called 'Findings') under the reporting procedure.

If the ECSR finds that the situation has been brought into conformity, the monitoring of the measures taken to follow up on the violation decision comes to an end. If, on the contrary, it finds that the situation is still not in conformity, the monitoring procedure continues, and the state will be required to submit information on these measures in the next report concerning the provision or provisions of the Charter whose violation has been highlighted in the decision on the merits.

It has also to be pointed out that the competence of the ECSR to monitor and assess follow-up to its violation decisions, provided for in Article 10 of the 1995 Protocol, was confirmed and enhanced by a decision of the Committee of Ministers in April 2014.[14] In this decision, with a view to simplifying the system of national reports for states having accepted the collective complaints procedure, the Committee of Ministers decided that monitoring of the follow-up to violation decisions adopted by the ECSR within the framework of the collective complaints procedure would be separated from the examination of 'ordinary' annual national reports. Accordingly, since 2015, every two years, instead of submitting an ordinary thematic report, the 15 states having ac-cepted the collective complaints procedure (16 States, from 2021), divided into

---

13. Article C of the Revised Charter, which reproduces, in this respect, Article 24 of the 1961 Charter, as amended by the Turin Protocol of 1991.
14. Decision adopted by the Committee of Ministers at the 1196th meeting of the minis-ters' deputies of 2 and 3 April 2014, entitled 'Ways of Streamlining and Improving the Reporting and Monitoring System of the European Social Charter', CM(2014)26.

two alternating groups, have been submitting a 'simplified' report, in which they describe solely what measures they have taken to follow up on the ECSR's violation decisions in collective complaints concerning them. And the ECSR adopts and publishes every two years, its 'Findings' as to whether the situation has been brought into conformity or not by the follow-up action by each state in the group in question.[15]

---

15. See, for example, 'Findings 2019' of the ECSR on follow-up by Croatia, Cyprus, the Czech Republic, the Netherlands, Norway, Slovenia and Sweden on decisions given in the context of the collective complaints procedure (https://rm.coe.int/follow-up-cc-2019-fr-findings-2019-on-the-follow-up-to-collective-comp/16809cf9a5).

Chapter 6

JURISDICTIONAL NATURE AND LEGAL VALUE OF THE ECSR'S DECISIONS ON THE MERITS

In light of the system of follow-up to violation decisions adopted by the European Committee of Social Rights (ECSR), it is possible to draw some conclusions about the legal value and actual impact of these decisions, and more generally about the importance and effectiveness of the collective complaints procedure as an instrument for protecting social rights in Europe.

From a 'formalistic' legal standpoint, it is all too clear that, despite the judicial character of the proceedings before the ECSR, the scrupulously adversarial nature of the procedure and the structure and contents of the ECSR's decisions, characterised by a painstaking analysis and description of all the factual and legal issues, a closely argued assessment and clear and precise operative provisions, the decisions on the merits of collective complaints are not tantamount to 'judgements' of an international court, that is, decisions with which the state in question is legally bound to comply. In fact, neither the 1995 Protocol nor the Revised Charter includes any provision identical or similar to Article 46 of the European Convention on Human Rights, as amended by Protocols 11 and 14 (or to Article 53 of the original 1950 version of the Convention).[1] The states parties to the 1995 Protocol are not formally bound, therefore, to comply with the Committee's decisions in cases to which they are party.

One could also express this in the following terms, namely, that when the ECSR adopts a decision on the merits of a collective complaint, it does not exercise a judicial function in the strict sense but a quasi-judicial function, and

---

1. Under Article 46, paragraph 1, of the ECHR: 'The High Contracting Parties undertake to abide by the *final judgment* of the Court in any case to which they are parties'. According to Article 53 of the 1950 Convention, 'The High Contracting Parties undertake to abide by *the decision* of the Court in any case to which they are parties' (emphasis added).

its decisions do not have the legal authority or status of *res judicata*, that is, the binding force of a court judgement.[2]

But setting aside general theoretical definitions and abstract legal classifications, and looking at the absence of binding force from the peculiar standpoint of international law, what such absence really implies is that if the state officials or organs concerned – whether they exercise legislative, executive, judicial or any other functions, whatever position they hold in the organisation of the state and whatever their character as an organ of the central government or of a territorial unit of the state[3] – fail to implement what is required to comply with an ECSR's violation decision, this would not, as such, constitute an infringement of an international obligation of the state concerned vis-à-vis other states parties to the 1995 Protocol. It would not be, therefore, an internationally wrongful act giving possibly rise, as a negative consequence, to the legitimate adoption of 'countermeasures' by another state party to the Protocol or the Committee of Ministers' adoption of 'sanctions', for example, the suspension of the state rights to participate in the activities of the Council of Europe or even its expulsion from the organisation.

There is no need, of course, either to underestimate or exaggerate the impact of such effects, arising from the international legally binding force of judgements of human rights courts (from the standpoint either of their preventive and dissuasive effectiveness or of their capacity to achieve an adequate implementation of human rights obligations).[4] It should, however, be noted that the fact that the ECSR's decisions on the merits are not legally binding – an aspect that makes them akin to the 'views' typical of certain UN treaty

---

2. This is, at least, the conclusion to be drawn if one accepts the theoretical approach of, *inter alios*, C. Santulli, 'Qu'est-ce qu'une juridiction internationale? Des organes répressifs internationaux à l'ORD', *Annuaire français de droit international*, 46 (2000): 58–81; H. Ascensio, 'La notion de juridiction internationale en question', in *Société Française de Droit international, La juridictionnalisation du droit international* (Paris: Pedone, 2003), 163–202; or Y. Kerbrat, 'Aspects de droit international général dans la pratique des comités établis au sein des Nations Unies dans le domaine des droits de l'homme 2008–2009', *Annuaire français de droit international*, 55 (2009), 699–713.

3. We refer here to the terminology used in Article 4 of the Draft Articles on 'Responsibility of States for Internationally Wrongful Acts', adopted by the United Nations International Law Commission, in order to determine the attribution of an internationally wrongful act to a state (the text of this provision and its commentary are available at https://legal.un.org/ilc/texts/instruments/english/commentaries/9_6_2001.pdf, at 40–42).

4. I do take account here, *mutatis mutandis*, of the reflections developed by Olivier Delas, Manon Thouvenot and Valérie Bergeron-Boutin, with reference to the decisions of the Human Rights Committee: O. Delas, M. Thouvenot and V. Bergeron-Boutin, 'Quelques considérations entourant la portée des décisions of Comité des Droits de l'Homme', *Revue québécoise de droit international*, 30, no. 2 (2017): 1–50, at 49–50.

bodies, such as the Human Rights Committee – is amply balanced by the fact that the states parties to the 1995 Protocol still consider themselves to be actually committed to take action to give effect to the ECSR's decision and thereby comply with their obligations under the Charter, in the specific situation that is the object of the collective complaint. They consider themselves so much committed to this that they have accepted, as noted, the (legally formal) obligation to submit regular reports to the ECSR on the measures taken to give effect to its decisions and bring the situation into conformity with the Charter.[5]

To continue with a 'formalistic' approach, one can therefore conclude that while, at the international level, decisions on the merits of collective complaints are not legally binding, because the states concerned are not obliged to comply with these decisions, they are not devoid of any legal effect. More precisely, the adoption of an ECSR's violation decision entails, firstly, an obligation on the part of the state concerned to report to the ECSR on the action taken to give effect to that decision and bring the situation into conformity with the Charter and, secondly, the possibility of 'soft-law sanctions', in the form of a Committee of Ministers recommendation addressed to the 'non-compliant' state.

Moreover, while it is clear from the 1995 Protocol that the states parties have not endowed collective complaints decisions on the merits with the legal force of *res judicata* in the substantial sense (*materielle Rechstkraft*), they did, nevertheless, want them to have the formal character of *res judicata* (*formelle Rechtskraft*): in other words, such decisions are final and become unchallengeable from the standpoint of the content of their legal assessment. This means that an ECSR's decision on the merits, once adopted, can no longer be modified either by another judicial or quasi-judicial body or by a political organ or institution, such as the Committee of Ministers. In fact, the Protocol makes no provision for any form of appeal against or revision of decisions on the merits of collective complaints, and the *Explanatory Report* states, quite unambiguously, that 'the Committee of Ministers cannot reverse the legal assessment made by the [ECSR]'.

It should also be borne in mind that the states parties to the 1995 Protocol have agreed to give the ECSR the *exclusive competence* to determine whether or not states have applied satisfactorily the Charter provision or provisions at

---

5. It should be added that, in their reports on follow-up to decisions on the merits of collective complaints, the states concerned, even if they have raised objections to the ECSR's assessment (and have challenged the violation decision in the Committee of Ministers), never question their obligation to give follow-up to such decisions and to bring the situation into compliance with the Charter, as indicated by the ECSR in its violation decision.

issue in collective complaints. The ECSR's decisions on the merits are therefore the only instrument that such states have accepted, and deem to be admissible, for securing at the international level a legal assessment of complaints or disputes concerning concrete and specific situations relating to compliance with obligations arising from the application of the European Social Charter (ESC).[6]

In conclusion, if one wanted to put the international legal nature of the ECSR's decisions on the merits in positive terms, one could say that they are jurisdictional decisions concerning the assessment of state compliance with ESC obligations called into question by a collective complaint and that they are decisions to which the states parties to the 1995 Protocol recognise a declaratory unchallengeable force, and to which the states concerned are obliged to give a follow-up by reporting back such follow-up to the ECSR to enable it to assess the measures taken in response to those decisions.[7]

This is much more appropriate and significant than simplistically concluding, in a purely negative way, that from an international standpoint these decisions are not 'court judgements' and do not have legally binding force.

---

6. This emerges clearly from Article 12 of the 1995 Protocol (and from the Appendix to Part III of the Revised Charter): 'It is understood that the Charter contains legal obligations of an international character, the application of which is submitted solely to the supervision provided for in Part IV thereof and in the provisions of this Protocol'.
7. This is again very similar, *mutatis mutandis*, to the conclusion already drawn by Olivier Delas, Manon Thouvenot and Valérie Bergeron-Boutin in their in-depth study on the decisions of the United Nations Human Rights Committee ('Quelques considérations entourant la portée des décisions du Comité des Droits de l'Homme'), 38–41.

Chapter 7

THE INTERPRETATIVE IMPORTANCE OF THE ECSR'S CASE LAW

Properly framing the European Committee of Social Rights' (ECSR's) decisions on the merits within the essentially jurisdictional context of the collective complaint procedure allows to understand their legal importance over and above the assessment of the specific case that is the object of a single collective complaint, namely, their importance from the more general perspective of identifying and interpreting the content of the obligations imposed on states by the European Social Charter (ESC).

It is of course correct to say that states parties to the 1995 Protocol, and thus also their domestic courts and tribunals and other state authorities and organs, are not legally bound to apply the ESC in accordance with the specific interpretation of the Charter's provisions given by the ECSR in its assessments under the collective complaints procedure.[1]

Nevertheless, the exclusive competence to monitor the implementation of the Charter from a *legal* standpoint, granted to the ECSR by the parties to

---

1. Of course, this is even more true in the case of states parties to the ESC that are not parties to the Protocol and to their courts and other relevant bodies. Moreover, the fact that, in international law, states parties to a treaty are under no obligation to comply with the 'pronouncements' of expert treaty bodies established under that treaty for the purposes of its interpretation has recently been underlined by the United Nations' International Law Commission (ILC) in its 'draft conclusions on subsequent agreements and subsequent practice in relation to the interpretation of treaties': see https://legal.un.org/ilc/texts/instruments/english/commentaries/1_11_2018.pdf. According to the ILC, these pronouncements cannot, in themselves, be considered to be 'expressions of the understanding of the treaty by the parties themselves' and do not, therefore, have the legal significance as authentic means of interpretation of the treaty, as is the case with subsequent agreements and subsequent practice: 'judgments and other pronouncements of international courts, tribunals and expert treaty bodies, however, may be indirectly relevant for the identification of subsequent agreements and subsequent practice as authentic means of interpretation if they reflect, give rise to or refer to such subsequent agreements and practice of the parties themselves' (commentary on Conclusion 3, paragraph 11' see also Conclusion 13 and its commentary).

the Charter system; the fact that the collective complaints procedure makes it possible to put the abstract normative prescriptions of the Social Charter to the test of specific and concrete situations; the judicial approach by which the Committee exercises its supervisory role under this procedure; the level of legal precision of its decisions on the merits; and the fact that, as already noted, the states concerned are actually committed to give a follow-up to such decisions, all help to give the ECSR's decisions an absolutely crucial interpretative value.[2]

More precisely, decisions on the merits, even though they lack the formally binding effect of *res interpretata*, can still serve to clarify, explain and supplement the content and implications of states' obligations as laid down in the Charter.

In other words, states parties to the Charter, including ones that are also party to the 1995 Protocol, are not legally bound to comply with the ECSR's interpretation of Charter provisions in its decisions on the merits of collective complaints when they – that is to say, their organs, including national judges and courts – are required to make domestic judicial rulings on Charter provisions, and they are not prevented from applying such provisions and rights on the basis of an alternative meaning or interpretation to that established in the ECSR's case law. Nevertheless, it is perfectly natural that the ECSR's consolidated case law (as emerging in its collective complaints decisions but also, of course, in its conclusions on state reports, under the reporting procedure)[3] indeed acts as the fundamental reference point, in all the states parties of the Charter system, for the implementation

---

2. See, in this regard, the response of the European Court of Human Rights to the United Kingdom's objection that 'the ECSR's assessment [was not] an authoritative source of law, since, despite the independence and expertise of its members, the ECSR did not possess judicial or quasi-judicial status. Its role was to report to the Committee of Ministers'. The Court observed that the ECSR's competence is stipulated in the Protocol amending the European Social Charter (also known as the 'Turin Protocol', Council of Europe Treaty Series No. 142), namely, to 'assess from a legal standpoint the compliance of national law and practice with the obligations arising from the Charter'. It is true that this Protocol has not come into force as several states parties to the Charter, including the United Kingdom, have not ratified it. *Yet the interpretative value of the ECSR appears to be generally accepted by states and by the Committee of Ministers. It is certainly accepted by the Court, which has repeatedly had regard to the ECSR's interpretation of the Charter and its assessment of state compliance with its various provisions. (National Union of Rail, Maritime and Transport Workers v. the United Kingdom*, complaint no. 31045/10, judgement of 8 April 2014, §94, emphasis added)

3. See Chapter 2, footnote 2.

and application (including domestic judicial application) of the Charter provisions.[4]

There are, in fact, significant examples of the substantive interpretative authority of decisions on the merits in several recent decisions in the domestic courts of states parties to the Charter. Such courts have made specific reference to ECSR's decisions and in so doing have ascribed to the relevant Charter provisions precisely the same content and scope as the ECSR had already given them in previous decisions. Moreover, this applies to judges, courts and tribunals, including constitutional courts, not only in state parties to the 1995 Protocol but also in states that have not accepted the collective complaints procedure.[5]

---

4. The interpretative value of the ECSR's jurisprudence therefore appears to come within the scope of what the International Court of Justice recognised (in the *Ahmadou Sadio Diallo* judgement) as being the legal importance of the case law of quasi-jurisdictional supervisory bodies, such as the Human Rights Committee or the African Commission on Human and Peoples' Rights. We would refer here to the most salient points made by the Hague Court (referring itself to the jurisprudence of the Human Rights Committee and the African Commission):

> [66] [...] Since it was created, the Human Rights Committee has built up a considerable body of interpretative case-law, in particular through its findings in response to the individual communications which may be submitted to it in respect of States parties to the first Optional Protocol, and in the form of its "General Comments". *Although the Court is in no way obliged, in the exercise of its judicial functions, to model its own interpretation of the Covenant on that of the Committee, it believes that it should ascribe great weight to the interpretation adopted by this independent body that was established specifically to supervise the application of that treaty. The point here is to achieve the necessary clarity and the essential consistency of international law, as well as legal security, to which both the individuals with guaranteed rights and the States obliged to comply with treaty obligations are entitled.* 67. Likewise, *when the Court is called upon, as in these proceedings, to apply a regional instrument for the protection of human rights, it must take due account of the interpretation of that instrument adopted by the independent bodies which have been specifically created, if such has been the case, to monitor the sound application of the treaty in question.* In the present case, the interpretation given above of Article 12, paragraph 4, of the African Charter is consonant with the case-law of the African Commission on Human and Peoples' Rights established by Article 30 of the said Charter. (Ahmadou Sadio Diallo case *(Republic of Guinea v. Democratic Republic of Congo)*, [2010] ICJ rec 639, §§66–67, emphasis added)

See also, on the legal authority of substantive interpretation of state obligations made by quasi-judicial human rights–monitoring bodies, the convincing arguments of D. Shelton, 'The Legal Status of Normative Pronouncements of Human Rights Treaty Bodies', in *Liber amicorum Rüdiger Wolfrum [Coexistence, Cooperation and Solidarity]*, ed. H. Hestermeyer et al. (Leiden-Boston: Martinus Nijhoff, 2012), 553–60.

5. The following may serve as examples. In Belgium, the Constitutional Court judgement of 27 July 2017, No. 101/2017, referred to the case law of the ECSR (in particular *Confédération française de l'Encadrement-CFE-CGC v. France*, complaint no. 16/2003, decision

Footnote: 5 (continued)

on the merits of 12 October 2004) to determine the content and implications of the right to strike under Article 6, paragraph 4, of the Charter, and the Brussels Labour Court, judgement of 13 May 2015, no. 2013/AB/614, referred to the *Conference of European Churches (CEC) v. The Netherlands*, complaint no. 90/2013, decision on the merits of 1 July 2014, and to *European Federation of National Organisations Working with the Homeless (FEANTSA) v The Netherlands*, complaint no. 86/2012, decision on the merits of 2 July 2014, to confirm the obligation to provide emergency assistance covering shelter, food, clothing and urgent medical care to migrants unlawfully present in the territory of the state, under Article 13 of the Charter.

The decision of 2 July 2014 on complaint no. 90/2013 (*Conference of European Churches v. The Netherlands*) was also referred to in the Netherlands by the Central Appeal Chamber (ECLI: NLCRVB 2014:4178, decision of 17 December 2014) and the Hague District Court (case No. AWB 14/8686, decision of 23 December 2014) to establish the scope of the obligations arising from Articles 13 and 31 of the Charter (ECLI: NLCRVB 2014:4178, decision of 17 December 2014).

In Italy, the Constitutional Court, in its judgement no. 194/2018 of 26 September 2018, referred explicitly to the Committee's case law (*Finnish Society of Social Rights v. Finland*, complaint no. 106/2014, decision on the admissibility and merits of 8 September 2016) to show that, in cases of termination of employment without valid reasons, any ceiling on compensation that may preclude damages from being commensurate with the loss suffered and from being sufficiently dissuasive is contrary to Article 24 of the Charter on the workers' right to protection in the case of termination of employment.

In France, two labour courts (Cons. Prud'h. Troyes 13-12-2018 No. 18/00036, Cons. Prud'h. Lyon 21-12-2018 No. 18/01238) relied on the same ECSR decision (*Finnish Society of Social Rights v. Finland*, complaint no. 106/2014) to find that the new scale of compensation for unfair dismissal introduced by the so-called Macron orders (order 2017–1387 of 22 September 2017) were incompatible with Article 24 of the ESC.

In Greece, in its judgement no. 3220/2017, the Piraeus Court of First Instance made explicit reference to the ECSR's case law on Article 24 of the Charter by stating that under this provision, as interpreted by the Committee, for a dismissal to be lawful, there must be valid grounds and that to be relied on in the court, such grounds must be proved by the employer. The Piraeus court also referred explicitly, in line with the position already taken by other Greek courts of first instance (Chios: judgement no. 37/2013, Xanthi: judgement no. 90/2013 and Patras: judgement no. 494/2013), to the 'interpretative authority' of ECSR decisions.

In Spain, which at that time was not a party to the 1995 collective complaints Protocol, Barcelona Labour Court No. 2 (judgement no. 412 of 19 November 2013) refused to abide by national legislation authorising dismissal of employees during their probationary periods without notice or compensation because the legislation was incompatible with Article 4, paragraph 4, of the Charter, as interpreted by the Committee in its decisions on the measures imposed on Greece by the so-called 'Troika' (*GENOP-DEI and ADEDY v. Greece*, complaint no. 65/2011, decisions on the merits of 23 May 2012). Several other Spanish labour courts have followed the lead of this judgement. A number of Spanish regional high courts have recently applied Article 4, paragraph 4, of the Charter in a similar fashion, by recognising that the ECSR case law must be taken into account as an 'authentic interpretation' of the Charter's provisions (see, in particular,

In short, in cases where obligations relating to social rights arising from Charter provisions have been the object of assessment in ECSR's decisions on the merits, such obligations end up assuming – for all the states parties to the Charter (and their organs and authorities, particularly their courts) – precisely the meaning and implications which have been established by the ECSR in its case law on relevant collective complaints.[6]

This indeed applies to a number of areas covered by the Charter, where the ECSR's decisions on the merits of collective complaints have established a significant body of case law clarifying the real meaning, implications and impact of Charter rights on many complex subject matters. These include: workers' right to a reasonable period of notice in the event of termination of employment and the right to social security in a time of 'austerity measures',[7] the right of employees dismissed for no valid reason to

---

the Canaries High Court, Las Palmas, Employment Bench, judgement no. 30/2016 of 28 January 2016, Rec. 581/2015; no. 252/2016 of 30 March 2016, Rec. 989/2015; no. 342/2016 of 18 April 2016, Rec. 110/2016; no. 1300/2016 of 31 January 2017).In Germany, another state that is not a party to the 1995 Protocol, the Constitutional Court also referred explicitly to the Committee's decisions concerning measures imposed on Greece by the 'Troika' (*GENOP-DEI and ADEDY v. Greece*, complaint no. 65/2011) to confirm, in accordance with this case law (§20 of the ECSR decision), that Article 1, paragraph 1, of the Charter concerned the achievement and maintenance of as high and stable a level of employment as possible, with a view to the attainment of full employment, but did not concern the protective provisions of labour and/or social security law (see BVerfG, Beschluss des Ersten Senats BvL 7/14, order of 6 June 2018).

6. On this, see also the study carried out by U. Khaliq and R. R. Churchill, 'The European Committee of Social Rights: Putting Flesh on the Bare Bones of the European Social Charter', in *Social Rights Jurisprudence: Emerging Trends in International and Comparative Law*, ed. M. Langford (Cambridge: Cambridge University Press, 2008), 428–52. It should be added that what also contributes to this general interpretative authority of decisions on the merits of collective complaints is the awareness of states parties to the Charter that applying a Charter provision in a manner that is incompatible with the Committee's case law could entail an 'indirect sanction' in the form of a conclusion of non-conformity adopted by the ECSR as part of the reporting procedure or a violation decision in the event of a collective complaint about a similar situation that has already been the object of a Committee decision on the merits.

7. *General Federation of Employees of the National Electric Power Corporation (GENOP-DEI)/ Confederation of Greek Civil Servants' Trade Unions (ADEDY) v. Greece*, complaint no. 65/ 2011, decision on the merits of 23 May 2012; *General Federation of Employees of the National Electric Power Corporation (GENOP-DEI)/Confederation of Greek Civil Servants' Trade Unions (ADEDY) v. Greece*, complaint no. 66/2011, decision on the merits of 23 May 2012; *Federation of Employed Pensioners of Greece (IKA–ETAM) v. Greece*, complaint no. 76/2012, decision on the merits of 7 December 2012; *Panhellenic Federation of Public Service Pensioners v. Greece*, complaint no. 77/2012, decision on the merits of 7 December 2012; *Pensioners' Union of the Athens-Piraeus Electric Railways (I.S.A.P.) v. Greece*, complaint no. 78/2012,

adequate and sufficiently dissuasive compensation,[8] education and vocational training for autistic children and children with other mental or intellectual disabilities,[9] the prohibition of all corporal punishment of children in the home or in school,[10] discrimination against Roma in various contexts,[11] entitlement to medical and social assistance and to emergency accommodation for unaccompanied foreign minors and for migrants unlawfully present in the

---

decision on the merits of 7 December 2012; *Panhellenic Federation of Pensioners of the Public Electricity Corporation (POS-DEI) v. Greece*, complaint no. 79/2012, decision on the merits of 7 December 2012; *Pensioners' Union of the Agricultural Bank of Greece (ATE) v. Greece*, complaint no. 80/2012, decision on the merits of 7 December 2012; *Greek General Confederation of Labour (GSEE) v. Greece*, complaint no. 111/2014, decision on the merits of 23 March 2017.

8. *Finnish Society of Social Rights v. Finland*, complaint no. 106/2014, decision on admissibility and merits of 8 September 2016; *Confederazione Generale Italiana del Lavoro (CGIL) v. Italy*, complaint no. 158/2017, of 11 September 2019.

9. *International Association Autism-Europe (IAAE) v. France*, complaint no. 13/2002, decision on the merits of 4 November 2003; *Mental Disability Advocacy Centre (MDAC) v. Bulgaria*, complaint no. 41/2007, decision on the merits of 3 June 2008; *International Federation of Human Rights (FIDH) v. Belgium*, complaint no. 75/2011, decision on the merits of 18 March 2013; *Action Européenne des Handicapés (AEH) v. France*, complaint no. 81/2012, decision on the merits of 11 September 2013; *Mental Disability Advocacy Centre (MDAC) v. Belgium*, complaint no. 109/2014, decision on admissibility and merits of 16 October 2017.

10. See the decisions on the merits adopted on 7 December 2004 on complaint nos. 17/2003 to 21/2003, lodged by the World Organisation against Torture (OMCT) against five states parties to the 1995 Protocol and the decisions on the merits adopted between September 2014 and January 2015 on complaint nos. 92/2013 to 98/2013 lodged by the Association for the Protection of All Children (APPROACH) against seven states parties to the 1995 Protocol.

11. *European Roma Rights Centre (ERRC) v. Greece*, complaint no. 15/2003, decision on the merits of 8 December 2004; *European Roma Rights Centre (ERRC) v. Bulgaria*, complaint no. 31/2005, decision on the merits of 18 October 2006; *European Roma Rights Centre (ERRC) v. Italy*, complaint no. 27/2004, decision on the merits of 7 December 2005; *European Roma Rights Centre (ERRC) v. France*, complaint no. 51/2008, decision on the merits of 19 October 2009; *Centre on Housing Rights and Evictions (COHRE) v. Italy*, complaint no. 58/2009, decision on the merits of 25 June 2010; *European Roma Rights Centre (ERRC) v. Portugal*, complaint no. 61/2010, decision on the merits of 2 November 2011; *Centre on Housing Rights and Evictions (COHRE) v. France*, complaint no. 63/2012, decision on the merits of 28 June 2011; *European Roma and Travellers Forum (ERTF) v. France*, complaint no. 64/2011, decision on the merits of 24 January 2012; *European Roma Rights Centre (ERRC) v. Ireland*, complaint no. 100/2013, decision on the merits of 1 December 2015; *European Roma and Travellers Forum (ERTF) v. Czech Republic*, complaint no. 104/2014, decision on the merits of 17 May 2016; *European Roma and Travellers Forum (ERTF) v. France*, complaint no. 119/2015, decision on the merits of 5 December 2017; *Equal Rights Trust v. Bulgaria*, complaint no. 121/2016, decision on the merits of 16 October

territory of the state,[12] the right to equal remuneration for equal or similar or comparable work between women and men[13] and the right to organise for military personnel and members of the police.[14]

2018; *European Roma Rights Centre (ERRC) v. Bulgaria*, complaint no. 151/2017, decision on the merits of 5 December 2018.

12. *Defence for Children International (DCI) v. The Netherlands*, complaint no. 47/2008, decision on the merits of 20 October 2009; *Defence for Children International (DCI) v. Belgium*, complaint no. 69/2011, decision on the merits of 23 October 2012; *European Federation of National Organisations Working with the Homeless (FEANTSA) v. The Netherlands*, complaint no. 86/2012, decision on the merits of 2 July 2014; *Conference of European Churches (CEC) v. The Netherlands*, complaint no. 90/2013, decision on the merits of 1 July 2014; *European Committee for Home-Based Priority Action for the Child and the Family (EUROCEF) v. France*, complaint no. 114/2015, decision on the merits of 24 January 2018.

13. See the 15 decisions on the merits adopted on 6 December 2019 on complaint nos. 124/2016 to 138/2016, lodged against all the states parties to the 1995 Protocol by University Women of Europe (UWE).

14. *European Council of Police Trade Unions v. Portugal*, complaint no. 11/2001, decision on the merits of 21 May 2012; *European Confederation of Police (EUROCOP) v. Ireland*, complaint no. 83/2012, decision on admissibility and merits of 2 December 2013; *European Council of Police Trade Unions (CESP) v. France*, complaint no. 101/2013, decision on the merits of 27 January 2016; *European Organisation of Military Associations (EUROMIL) v. Ireland*, complaint no. 112/2014, decision on the merits of 12 September 2017; *Confederazione Generale Italiana del Lavoro (CGIL) v. Italy*, complaint no. 140/2016, decisions on the merits of 22 January 2019; *Unione Generale Lavoratori – Federazione Nazionale Corpo forestale dello Stato (UGL–CFS) and Sindacato autonomo polizia ambientale forestale (SAPAF) v. Italy*, complaint no. 143/2017, decision on the merits of 3 July 2019.

Chapter 8

FINAL CONSIDERATIONS: EFFECTIVENESS AND APPROPRIATENESS OF THE COLLECTIVE COMPLAINTS PROCEDURE AS AN INSTRUMENT FOR PROTECTING SOCIAL RIGHTS IN EUROPE

Having examined the legal nature and value of the European Committee of Social Rights' (ECSR's) decisions on the merits, it is now time to consider the actual effectiveness of the quasi-jurisdictional monitoring activity carried out by the ECSR in the collective complaints procedure, that is, the extent to which its monitoring has a real impact on situations that are the object of complaints, in the sense of securing greater respect for social rights obligations by the European states concerned.

From this standpoint, it certainly cannot be said that the collective complaints procedure always – or even usually – results in resolution of the problem at stake, with the national situation concerned brought fully and rapidly into line with the Charter's requirements, in terms of social rights protection.

There are in fact many cases where, even after repeated findings of violation by the ECSR, the situation of non-compliance with the Charter continues to go unremedied for several years, and the state concerned fails to respond and take remedial action. This clearly emerges, unfortunately, from the ECSR's annual 'Findings' on states' follow-up to violation decisions affecting them.

Nevertheless, there are also numerous examples of states that have spontaneously and quite rapidly reacted to ECSR's violation decisions, by taking steps and measures to rectify or improve the situation, in order to bring it into conformity with the Charter provisions. And in a large majority of cases, the fact that a collective complaint has been submitted to the ECSR and that the

Committee has adopted a violation decision still appears to be an important factor in the state's positive change of attitude – in terms of social rights implementation – in respect of the situation that was highlighted by the complaint.

As explained above, once the ECSR has adopted a violation decision, it continues to monitor the situation, and the state concerned must regularly report to it on the measures eventually taken to give effect to the decision. This clearly helps to ensure that states that are the addressees of ECSR's violation decision do not remain inactive but somehow undertake to bring the situation more into line with the Charter's requirements.

However, we believe that other factors are still more important in making the collective complaints procedure a suitable instrument for securing the effective implementation of the rights enshrined in the Charter.

Firstly, this procedure opens the door of the Social Charter to the civil society, to NGOs and to the world of workers. This means opening the European system for the protection of social rights to those whom it benefits directly and who – more than states and governments – have an interest in the application and effective enjoyment of these rights. Secondly, there is the 'publicity factor', determined by the fact that not only the complaints lodged but also other documents and files produced during the proceedings, as well as the ECSR's violation decisions, all become published and readily accessible material, which are endowed with the remarkable public impact typical of the Council of Europe acts and initiatives.[1]

These two factors – the fact that complainant organisations are collective bodies and important representatives of organised civil society and organised labour and that the ECSR's proceedings and decisions are widely publicised and disseminated – clearly interact to produce an effective form of social pressure on governments, legislators and other national authorities to alter their

---

1. As regards the importance of the 'publicity action' (*action de publicité*) as a major assurance on the effective implementation of states' international obligations on human rights, we would simply recall the words of Jean Charpentier:

It is hard to overestimate the importance of publicity in the application of international law. Its effect is clearly linked to that of public opinion, since its purpose is to alert the latter so that it can, in turn, persuade those that govern us to alter their conduct. Its effectiveness depends, therefore, on public awareness of international problems, since this alone can stimulate a public demand for action, and on the existence of democratic institutions that offer the public the legal means to oblige governments to take account of its demands. The fact of publicising violations and failings is perhaps more important than the initial finding. (J. Charpentier, 'Le contrôle par les organisations internationales de l'exécution des obligations des Etats', in *Recueil des cours de l'Académie de Droit international de la Haye*, 182 (1983-IV), 221–22, author's translation).

conduct to come into line with the requirements of the Charter, as interpreted by the ECSR.

By contrast, a factor of weakness from the standpoint of the procedure's effectiveness is the lack of international political weight attached to the ECSR's decisions, as reflected in the lukewarm reception they receive from the Council of Europe's Committee of Ministers and national delegations participating in this Committee. Thus, the Committee of Ministers does not, in practice, play the active role vested in it by the 1995 Protocol. More specifically, it has almost never used its powers/duties under Article 9, paragraph 1, of the Protocol to address recommendations to states parties found by the ECSR to be in violation of the Charter.[2] Moreover, it is very rare for other Council of Europe member states to invite or urge a fellow member state to respond to or take action on an ECSR decision on the merits.

To increase the effectiveness of the Charter system, therefore, the Committee of Ministers should be more sensitive to the fact that the ESC and its supervisory body, the ECSR, are an asset shared by all the Council of Europe member states and that they should unite their efforts to ensure that the Charter and the ECSR's decisions are fully respected. Peer pressure exerted by other states parties, and by the Council of Europe's main governing body, would go a very long way to increasing the effectiveness of the collective complaints procedure.

Finally, there is an intrinsic limit to the effectiveness of the collective complaints procedure which must be taken into account. We are referring precisely to its *collective nature*,[3] that is, to the fact that it is neither designed nor intended to deal with the violation of the rights of individuals. The ECSR's decisions are therefore unable to require states to re-establish the rights of single individuals or remedy the prejudice suffered by individually identified victims.

This is the major difference between the collective complaints procedure and other human rights–monitoring mechanisms providing for individual applications or complaints to international judicial or quasi-jurisdictional bodies. As is well known, such mechanisms are mostly in force and active in the field of civil and political rights (e.g. applications to the European Court of Human Rights or individual communications to the Human Rights Committee), but they also exist in the economic and social rights field, as in the case of the Optional Protocol to the International Covenant on Economic, Social and Cultural

---

2. As noted above, fortunately such an approach by the Committee of Ministers seems to be changing recently (see Chapter 5, footnote 10).
3. See Chapter 2.

Rights[4] and the Additional 'San Salvador' Protocol to the American Convention on Human Rights,[5] which provides for individual applications in respect of violations of trade union rights and the right to education.

But to what extent does this intrinsic limitation on the Charter system's complaints procedure really pose a problem for the effective protection of social rights?

At least two aspects of the ESC system may indeed make the exclusively collective – as opposed to individual – nature of complaints less of a shortcoming than might appear.

Firstly, one has to consider that a large majority of the social rights provisions in the ESC are formulated in terms of states' positive obligations and general commitments, rather than obligations to respect or ensure individuals' subjective rights. This makes it unlikely that individuals could claim themselves to be (or be recognised as such by the competent supervisory body) as 'victims' of a violation, that is, persons whose subjective rights have been infringed directly as a result of state conduct incompatible with the Charter.

The other aspect is that if international bodies are to *effectively* protect *individual rights*, they require, even more than the power to oversee the implementation of states' obligations, the assurance that their decisions will have binding legal force not only at the international level but also at the domestic level, requiring state authorities and organs (particularly the judiciary) to restore the rights of the individuals concerned and/or award them just satisfaction. This is, in fact, what characterises systems instituting genuine human rights courts, such as those established by the European and American human rights conventions, but not, as already noted, the ESC and its supervisory body, the ECSR (or, for that matter, the two international covenants and their respective supervisory bodies).

In other words, the fact that the Charter system fails to provide for the binding legal force of ECSR decisions (at both international and domestic levels) means that any protective system incorporating the right of individual application (or complaint) would still not be fully effective.

For both the above reasons, the fact that the ESC system is not empowered to deal with individuals' claims and violations of rights suffered by individuals does not constitute a major impediment to safeguarding the rights embodied in the Charter. Or to be more accurate, given the content of the Charter's provisions, the nature of its supervisory body and the non-legally binding force of its decisions, it would have been less effective in offering protection of social

---

4. Optional Protocol to the International Covenant on Economic, Social and Cultural Rights of 10 December 2008, entered into force on 5 May 2013. Twenty-four states parties to the Covenant are also parties to the Protocol.

5. Additional Protocol to the American Convention on Human Rights in the Area of Economic, Social and Cultural Rights, 'Protocol of San Salvador', adopted in San Salvador on 17 November 1988, entered into force on 16 November 1999.

rights if an individual complaints mechanism had been instituted, as a monitoring mechanism, in place of the existing collective complaints procedure.

A further consideration can be made to confirm this point.

It is true that even a non-jurisdictional machinery for individual applications can potentially achieve in putting pressure on the state concerned to restore the enjoyment of rights of individual victims of social rights violations and redress the damages suffered by them, though the effects would be confined to the individual situation that was the object of the application. However, it is also true that such a machinery would be very unlikely to secure the most important outcome from the standpoint of actually implementing the kind of rights enshrined in the Charter, namely, inducing states to resolve systemic and structural problems, obstacles and shortcomings that prevent the general and effective enjoyment of social rights by all the people living within their jurisdiction.

The collective complaints procedure, on the other hand, as provided for in the 1995 Protocol and applied in practice by the ECSR, is designed precisely to uncover and resolve systemic and structural problems relating to specific – but general (in the sense of non-individual) – situations and to put pressure on states to tackle and remedy these problems, under the continuing supervision of the ECSR, for the benefit not only of any eventual victims of the specific violation on which the complaint is based but also of all those members of the community with an interest in the implementation of the social rights in question.

Obviously, none of what has been said above alters the fact that it would still be useful and appropriate to have, at the European level, a petition machinery – possibly of a judicial nature – tasked with addressing alleged violations of individuals' social rights by states. Such a machinery institution would clearly take as its model the example and experience of the European Court of Human Rights (before or after the reform of Protocol 11 to the Convention).

However, this should not be at the cost of sacrificing or radically changing the collective complaints procedure laid down by the 1995 Protocol, which in its more than two decades of existence has proved to be an appropriate and effective instrument for protecting and safeguarding social rights in Europe.

Such procedure should not only continue to function but also be strengthened and applied more widely. This is, moreover, the wish of, among others, the Secretary General[6] and the Committee of Ministers[7] of the Council of

---

6. See the 2019 report of the Secretary General for the ministerial session in Helsinki, 16–17 May 2019: 'Ready for Future Challenges – Reinforcing the Council of Europe', https://rm.coe.int/CoERMPublicCommonSearchServices/DisplayDCTMCont ent?documentId=090000168093af03, 34–35.

7. Decision of the Committee of Ministers of the Council of Europe, adopted at the 129th session (Helsinki, May 2019), CM/Del/Dec(2019)129/2a, https://search.coe.int/cm/ pages/result_details.aspx?objectid=09000016809477f1, cited in 'Introduction', footnote 8.

Europe, the states parties to the 1995 Protocol[8] and even the relevant depart-
ments of the European Commission of the European Union (in the context
of their work on implementing the European Pillar of Social Rights),[9] all of
whom have recently stressed the importance of this procedure's acceptance by
European states that have not already done so.

---

8. See the 'Call by the representatives of the 15 states parties to the European Social
   Charter having accepted the 1995 Additional Protocol and the collective complaints
   procedure to reinforce social rights protection in Europe' launched following the sem-
   inar 'Reinforcing Social Rights Protection in Europe to Achieve Greater Unity and
   Equality', organised under the auspices of the French chairmanship (see https://
   rm.coe.int/call-by-the-representatives-of-the-15-states-parties-to-the-esc-for-ac/168
   0983870).
9. See the Commission staff working document accompanying the document 'Monitoring
   the Implementation of the European Pillar of Social Rights' (cited by O. De Schutter,
   *The European Pillar of Social Rights and the Role of the European Social Charter in the EU Legal
   Order*, see 'Introduction', footnote 3), which states 'implementation of the pillar could be
   reinforced by ratifying relevant ILO conventions, the Revised European Social Charter
   of 1996 and its Additional Protocol Providing for a System of Collective Complaints'.

BIBLIOGRAPHY

Akandji-Kombé, Jean-François, and Leclerc, Stéphane (eds). *La Charte Sociale Européenne*. Brussels: Bruylant, 2001.

Alston, Philip. 'Assessing the Strengths and Weaknesses of the European Social Charter's Supervisory System', in *Social Rights in Europe*, ed. B. De Burca and B. De Witte. Oxford: Oxford University Press, 2005, 45–68.

Ascensio, Hervé. 'La notion de juridiction internationale en question', in *Société Française de Droit international, La juridictionnalisation du droit international*. Paris: Pedone, 2003, 163–202.

Barile, Giuseppe. 'La Carta sociale europea e il diritto internazionale', *Rivista di diritto internazionale*, 44, no. 4 (1961): 629–44.

Belorgey, Jean-Michel. 'La Carta social europea y el Comité europeo de derechos sociales: el mecanismo de reclamaciones colectivas', in *Tratado sobre Protección de Derechos Sociales*, ed. M. Terol Becerra and L. Jimena Quesada. Valencia: Tirant, 2014, 231–48.

Benelhocine, Carole. *La Charte Sociale Européenne*. Strasbourg: Editions du Conseil de l'Europe, 2011.

Brillat, Régis. 'The Supervisory Machinery of the European Social Charter: Recent Developments and Their Impact', in *Social Rights in Europe*, ed. B. De Burca and B. De Witte. Oxford: Oxford University Press, 2005, 11–44.

Bruun, Niklas G., Lörcher, Klaus, Schömann, Isabelle, and Clauwaert, Stefan (eds). *The European Social Charter and the Employment Relation*. Oxford: Hart, 2017.

Charpentier, Jean. 'Le contrôle par les organisations internationales de l'exécution des obligations des Etats', in *Recueil des cours de l'Académie de Droit international de la Haye*, 182 (1983-IV), 143–245.

Churchill, Robin R., and Khaliq, Urfan. 'The Collective Complaint Mechanism for Ensuring Compliance with Economic and Social Rights: An Effective Mechanism for Ensuring Compliance with Economic and Social Rights?', *European Journal of International Law*, 15, no. 3 (2004): 417–56.

———. 'Violations of Economic, Social and Cultural Rights: The Current Use and Future Potential of the Collective Complaints Mechanism of the European Social Charter', in *Economic, Social and Cultural Rights in Action*, ed. M. Baderin and R. McCorquodale. Oxford: Oxford University Press, 2007, 195–240.

Clauwaert, Stefan. 'The Charter's Supervisory Procedures', in *The European Social Charter and the Employment Relation*, ed. N. G. Bruun et al. Oxford: Hart, 2017, 99–144.

Coomans, Fons (ed.). *Justiciability of Economic and Social Rights: Experiences from Domestic Systems*. Antwerp: Intersentia, 2006.

Cullen, Holly. 'The Collective Complaints System of the European Social Charter: Interpretative Methods of the European Committee of Social Rights', *Human Rights Law Review*, 9, no. 1 (2009), 61–93.

Delas, Olivier, Thouvenot, Manon, and Bergeron-Boutin, Valérie. 'Quelques considérations entourant la portée des décisions of Comité des Droits de l'Homme', *Revue québécoise de droit international*, 30, no. 2 (2017), 1–50.

De Schutter, Olivier (ed.). *The European Social Charter: A Social Constitution for Europe*. Brussels: Bruylant, 2010.

Dörr, Oliver. 'European Social Charter', in *The Council of Europe: Its Laws and Policies*, ed. S. Schmahl and M. Breuer. Oxford: Oxford University Press, 2017, 507–41.

Gernigon, B. 'La protection de la liberté syndicale par l'OIT: une expérience de cinquante années', *Revue belge de droit international*, 33, no. 1 (2000), 12–25.

Harris, D. J. 'The European Social Charter', *International and Comparative Law Quarterly*, 13, no. 3 (1964): 1076–87.

Harris, David J., and Darcy, John. *The European Social Charter*, 2nd edition. Ardsley, NY: Transnational Publishers, 2001.

Kerbrat, Yves. 'Aspects de droit international général dans la pratique des comités établis au sein des Nations Unies dans le domaine des droits de l'homme 2008–2009', *Annuaire français de droit international*, 55 (2009), 699–713.

Khaliq, Urfan, and Churchill, Robin R. 'The European Committee of Social Rights. Putting Flesh on the Bare Bones of the European Social Charter', in *Social Rights Jurisprudence. Emerging Trends in International and Comparative Law*, ed. M. Langford. Cambridge: Cambridge University Press, 2008, 428–52.

Lukas, Karin. 'The Collective Complaints Procedure of the European Social Charter', *Legal Issues of Economic Integration*, 41, no. 3 (2014): 275–88.

———. *The Revised European Social Charter. An Article by Article Commentary*. Cheltenham: Edward Elgar, 2021.

Luther, Jörg, and Lorenza, Mola (eds). *Les droits sociaux de l'Europe sous le 'processus de Turin' [Europe's Social Rights under the 'Turin Process']*. Napoli: Editoriale scientifica, 2016.

Mapulanga-Hulston, Jackbeth K. 'Examining the Justiciability of Economic, Social and Cultural Rights', *International Journal of Human Rights*, 6, no. 4 (Winter 2002), 29–48.

Mikkola, Matti. *Social Human Rights of Europe*. Porvoo: Karelactio, 2010.

Novitz, Tonia A. 'Are Social Rights Necessarily Collective Rights? A Critical Analysis of the Collective Complaints Protocol to the European Social Charter', *European Human Rights Law Review*, no. 1 (2002): 50–66.

Palmisano, Giuseppe. 'Overcoming the Limits of the European Social Charter in Terms of Persons Protected: The Case of Third State Nationals and Irregular Migrants', in *La Charte Sociale Européenne et les défis du XXIe siècle [European Social Charter and the Challenges of the Twenty-First Century]*, ed. M. D'Amico and G. Guiglia. Napoli: Edizioni scientifiche italiane, 2014, 171–91.

———. 'La procédure de réclamations collectives en tant qu'instrument de protection internationale des droits sociaux', *Revue Générale de droit International Public*, 124, nos. 3–4 (2020): 513–63.

Priore, Riccardo. 'Les systèmes de contrôle de l'application de la Charte sociale européenne: la procédure de réclamations collectives', in *La Charte Sociale Européenne et les défis du XXIe siècle [European Social Charter and the Challenges of the Twenty-First Century]*, ed. M. D'Amico and G. Guiglia. Napoli: Edizioni scientifiche italiane, 2014, 159–70.

Santulli, Carlo. 'Qu'est-ce qu'une juridiction internationale? Des organes répressifs internationaux à l'ORD', *Annuaire français de droit international*, 46 (2000): 58–81.

Shelton, Dinah. 'The Legal Status of Normative Pronouncements of Human Rights Treaty Bodies', in *Liber amicorum Rüdiger Wolfrum [Coexistence, Cooperation and Solidarity]*, ed. H. Hestermeyer et al. Leiden-Boston: Martinus Nijhoff, 2012, 553–60.

Sudre, Frédéric. 'Le Protocole additionnel à la Charte sociale européenne prévoyant un système de réclamations collectives', *Revue générale de droit international public*, 100, no. 3 (1996): 715–39.

Świątkowski, Andrzej. *The Charter of Social Rights of the Council of Europe*. Alphen a/d Rijn: Kluwer Law International, 2007.

Valticos, Nicolas. 'La Charte sociale européenne: sa structure, son contenu, le contrôle de son application', *Droit social*, 26, September/October (1963): 466–82.

Wiebringhaus, Hans. 'La Charte sociale européenne', *Annuaire français de droit international*, 9 (1963): 709–21.

INDEX

CPSIA information can be obtained
at www.ICGtesting.com
Printed in the USA
BVHW041723241022
650027BV00001B/83